TABLE OF CONTENTS

Success Strategies

This section contains a list of test-taking strategies that you may find helpful as you work through the test. By taking what you know and applying logical thought, you can maximize your chances of answering any question correctly!

It is very important to realize that every question is different and every person is different: no single strategy will work on every question, and no single strategy will work for every person. That's why we've included all of them here, so you can try them out and determine which ones work best for different types of questions and which ones work best for you.

Question Strategies

Read Carefully

Read the question and answer choices carefully. Don't miss the question because you misread the terms. You have plenty of time to read each question thoroughly and make sure you understand what is being asked. Yet a happy medium must be attained, so don't waste too much time. You must read carefully, but efficiently.

Contextual Clues

Look for contextual clues. If the question includes a word you are not familiar with, look at the immediate context for some indication of what the word might mean. Contextual clues can often give you all the information you need to decipher the meaning of an unfamiliar word. Even if you can't determine the meaning, you may be able to narrow down the possibilities enough to make a solid guess at the answer to the question.

Prefixes

If you're having trouble with a word in the question or answer choices, try dissecting it. Take advantage of every clue that the word might include. Prefixes and suffixes can be a huge help. Usually they allow you to determine a basic meaning. Pre- means before, post- means after, pro - is positive, de- is negative. From prefixes and suffixes, you can get an idea of the general meaning of the word and try to put it into context.

Hedge Words

Watch out for critical hedge words, such as *likely, may, can, sometimes, often, almost, mostly, usually, generally, rarely,* and *sometimes.* Question writers insert these hedge phrases to cover every possibility. Often an answer choice will be wrong simply because it leaves no room for exception. Be on guard for answer choices that have definitive words such as *exactly* and *always.*

Switchback Words

Stay alert for *switchbacks.* These are the words and phrases frequently used to alert you to shifts in thought. The most common switchback words are *but, although,* and *however.* Others include *nevertheless, on the other hand, even though, while, in spite of, despite, regardless of.* Switchback words are important to catch because they can change the direction of the question or an answer choice.

Face Value

When in doubt, use common sense. Accept the situation in the problem at face value. Don't read too much into it. These problems will not require you to make wild assumptions. If you have to go beyond creativity and warp time or space in order to have an answer choice fit the question, then you should move on and consider the other answer choices. These are normal problems rooted in reality. The applicable relationship or explanation may not be readily apparent, but it is there for you to figure out. Use your common sense to interpret anything that isn't clear.

Answer Choice Strategies

Answer Selection

The most thorough way to pick an answer choice is to identify and eliminate wrong answers until only one is left, then confirm it is the correct answer. Sometimes an answer choice may immediately seem right, but be careful. The test writers will usually put more than one reasonable answer choice on each question, so take a second to read all of them and make sure that the other choices are not equally obvious. As long as you have time left, it is better to read every answer choice than to pick the first one that looks right without checking the others.

Answer Choice Families

An answer choice family consists of two (in rare cases, three) answer choices that are very similar in construction and cannot all be true at the same time. If you see two answer choices that are direct opposites or parallels, one of them is usually the correct answer. For instance, if one answer choice says that quantity x increases and another either says that quantity x decreases (opposite) or says that quantity y increases (parallel), then those answer choices would fall into the same family. An answer choice that doesn't match the construction of the answer choice family is more likely to be incorrect. Most questions will not have answer choice families, but when they do appear, you should be prepared to recognize them.

Eliminate Answers

Eliminate answer choices as soon as you realize they are wrong, but make sure you consider all possibilities. If you are eliminating answer choices and realize that the last one you are left with is also wrong, don't panic. Start over and consider each choice again. There may be something you missed the first time that you will realize on the second pass.

Avoid Fact Traps

Don't be distracted by an answer choice that is factually true but doesn't answer the question. You are looking for the choice that answers the question. Stay focused on what the question is asking for so you don't accidentally pick an answer that is true but incorrect. Always go back to the question and make sure the answer choice you've selected actually answers the question and is not merely a true statement.

Extreme Statements

In general, you should avoid answers that put forth extreme actions as standard practice or proclaim controversial ideas as established fact. An answer choice that states the "process should be used in certain situations, if..." is much more likely to be correct than one that states the "process should be discontinued completely." The first is a calm rational statement and doesn't even make a definitive, uncompromising stance, using a hedge word *if* to provide wiggle room, whereas the second choice is a radical idea and far more extreme.

Benchmark

As you read through the answer choices and you come across one that seems to answer the question well, mentally select that answer choice. This is not your final answer, but it's the one that will help you evaluate the other answer choices. The one that you selected is your benchmark or standard for judging each of the other answer choices. Every other answer choice must be compared to your benchmark. That choice is correct until proven otherwise by another answer choice beating it. If you find a better answer, then that one becomes your new benchmark. Once you've decided that no other choice answers the question as well as your benchmark, you have your final answer.

Predict the Answer

Before you even start looking at the answer choices, it is often best to try to predict the answer. When you come up with the answer on your own, it is easier to avoid distractions and traps because you will know exactly what to look for. The right answer choice is unlikely to be word-for-word what you came up with, but it should be a close match. Even if you are confident that you have the right answer, you should still take the time to read each option before moving on.

General Strategies

Tough Questions

If you are stumped on a problem or it appears too hard or too difficult, don't waste time. Move on! Remember though, if you can quickly check for obviously incorrect answer choices, your chances of guessing correctly are greatly improved. Before you completely give up, at least try to knock out a couple of possible answers. Eliminate what you can and then guess at the remaining answer choices before moving on.

Check Your Work

Since you will probably not know every term listed and the answer to every question, it is important that you get credit for the ones that you do know. Don't miss any questions through careless mistakes. If at all possible, try to take a second to look back over your answer selection and make sure you've selected the correct answer choice and haven't made a costly careless mistake (such as marking an answer choice that you didn't mean to mark). This quick double check should more than pay for itself in caught mistakes for the time it costs.

Pace Yourself

It's easy to be overwhelmed when you're looking at a page full of questions; your mind is confused and full of random thoughts, and the clock is ticking down faster than you would like. Calm down and maintain the pace that you have set for yourself. Especially as you get down to the last few minutes of the test, don't let the small numbers on the clock make you panic. As long as you are on track by monitoring your pace, you are guaranteed to have time for each question.

Don't Rush

It is very easy to make errors when you are in a hurry. Maintaining a fast pace in answering questions is pointless if it makes you miss questions that you would have gotten right otherwise. Test writers like to include distracting information and wrong answers that seem right. Taking a little extra time to avoid careless mistakes can make all the difference in your test score. Find a pace that allows you to be confident in the answers that you select.

Keep Moving

Panicking will not help you pass the test, so do your best to stay calm and keep moving. Taking deep breaths and going through the answer elimination steps you practiced can help to break through a stress barrier and keep your pace.

Final Notes

The combination of a solid foundation of content knowledge and the confidence that comes from practicing your plan for applying that knowledge is the key to maximizing your performance on test day. As your foundation of content knowledge is built up and strengthened, you'll find that the strategies included in this chapter become more and more effective in helping you quickly sift through the distractions and traps of the test to isolate the correct answer.

Now it's time to move on to the test content chapters of this book, but be sure to keep your goal in mind. As you read, think about how you will be able to apply this information on the test. If you've already seen sample questions for the test and you have an idea of the question format and style, try to come up with questions of your own that you can answer based on what you're reading. This will give you valuable practice applying your knowledge in the same ways you can expect to on test day.

Good luck and good studying!

Chapter 1 - Whole Numbers

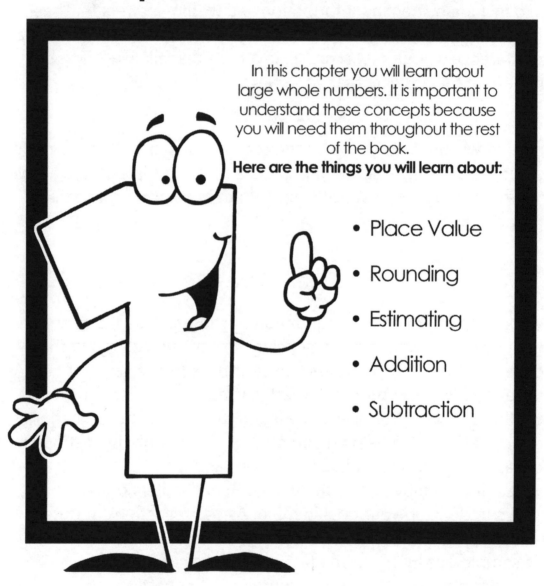

In this chapter you will learn about large whole numbers. It is important to understand these concepts because you will need them throughout the rest of the book.

Here are the things you will learn about:

- Place Value

- Rounding

- Estimating

- Addition

- Subtraction

Lesson 1

Place Value 1-10,000,000

The place value of a digit is determined by where it is in a number.

Ten Millions	Millions	Hundred Thousands	Ten Thousands	Thousands	Hundreds	Tens	Ones
1	2	3	4	5	6	7	8

12,345,678

Twelve million, three hundred forty-five thousand, six hundred seventy-eight

Match the numbers below to the correct place value boxes.

1. 15,632,782 =

1	5	6	3	2	7	8	2
Ten Millions	Millions	Hundred Thousands	Ten Thousands	Thousands	Hundreds	Tens	Ones

2. 24,879,360 =

Ten Millions	Millions	Hundred Thousands	Ten Thousands	Thousands	Hundreds	Tens	Ones

3. 62,158,524 =

Ten Millions	Millions	Hundred Thousands	Ten Thousands	Thousands	Hundreds	Tens	Ones

4. 30,671,234 =

Ten Millions	Millions	Hundred Thousands	Ten Thousands	Thousands	Hundreds	Tens	Ones

5. 52,197,305 =

Ten Millions	Millions	Hundred Thousands	Ten Thousands	Thousands	Hundreds	Tens	Ones

6. 83,498,147 =

Ten Millions	Millions	Hundred Thousands	Ten Thousands	Thousands	Hundreds	Tens	Ones

Place Value 1-100,000,000

The place value of a digit is determined by where it is in a number.

Hundred Millions	Ten Millions	Millions	Hundred Thousands	Ten Thousands	Thousands	Hundreds	Tens	Ones
1	2	3	4	5	6	7	8	9

123,456,789

One hundred twenty-three million, four hundred fifty-six thousand, seven hundred eighty-nine

Match the numbers below to the correct place value boxes.

1. 748,422,719 =

Hundred Millions	Ten Millions	Millions	Hundred Thousands	Ten Thousands	Thousands	Hundreds	Tens	Ones

2. 329,608,114 =

Hundred Millions	Ten Millions	Millions	Hundred Thousands	Ten Thousands	Thousands	Hundreds	Tens	Ones

3. 124,375,277 =

Hundred Millions	Ten Millions	Millions	Hundred Thousands	Ten Thousands	Thousands	Hundreds	Tens	Ones

4. 741,588,379 =

Hundred Millions	Ten Millions	Millions	Hundred Thousands	Ten Thousands	Thousands	Hundreds	Tens	Ones

5. 504,267,332 =

Hundred Millions	Ten Millions	Millions	Hundred Thousands	Ten Thousands	Thousands	Hundreds	Tens	Ones

6. 972,114,089 =

Hundred Millions	Ten Millions	Millions	Hundred Thousands	Ten Thousands	Thousands	Hundreds	Tens	Ones

Lesson 2

Rounding up to 100,000

Round the following numbers to the nearest thousand.

1.	2,563 _____3,000_____	**6.**	4,219 _____
2.	9,198 _____	**7.**	5,756 _____
3.	1,423 _____	**8.**	8,154 _____
4.	7,712 _____	**9.**	6,069 _____
5.	3,300 _____	**10**	1,995 _____

Round the following numbers to the nearest ten-thousand.

11.	39,092 _____	**16.**	77,150 _____
12.	19,917 _____	**17.**	33,809 _____
13.	93,254 _____	**18.**	35,451 _____
14.	56,055 _____	**19.**	20,901 _____
15.	70,856 _____	**20.**	48,599 _____

Round the following numbers to the nearest hundred-thousand.

21.	274,333 _____	**26.**	317,110 _____
22.	596,559 _____	**27.**	882,658 _____
23.	221,324 _____	**28.**	610,567 _____
24.	530,708 _____	**29.**	789,381 _____
25.	189,365 _____	**30.**	109,277 _____

Lesson 3

Building Numbers

Use what you learned about place value to sort and solve the problems below.

1. $3 + 400 + 4,000 + 20,000 + 50 = \underline{2\,4,4\,5\,3}$ **2.** $50,000 + 700 + 10 + 5,000 + 8 = \underline{\hphantom{0000}}$

3. $500 + 50 + 10,000 + 9,000 + 4 = \underline{\hphantom{0000}}$ **4.** $8,000 + 100 + 30 + 2 + 20,000 = \underline{\hphantom{0000}}$

5. $10,000 + 900 + 60 + 2,000 + 6 = \underline{\hphantom{0000}}$ **6.** $90,000 + 300 + 50 + 9 + 3,000 = \underline{\hphantom{0000}}$

7. $1 + 500 + 6,000 + 90,000 + 90 = \underline{\hphantom{0000}}$ **8.** $700 + 70 + 50,000 + 6,000 + 2 = \underline{\hphantom{0000}}$

9. $3,000 + 200 + 90 + 7 + 80,000 = \underline{\hphantom{0000}}$ **10.** $5 + 900 + 7,000 + 20,000 + 10 = \underline{\hphantom{0000}}$

11. $5,000 + 200 + 10 + 2 + 30,000 = \underline{\hphantom{0000}}$ **12.** $600 + 80 + 60,000 + 2,000 + 9 = \underline{\hphantom{0000}}$

13. $40,000 + 200 + 10 + 9,000 + 2 = \underline{\hphantom{0000}}$ **14.** $9,000 + 300 + 50 + 9 + 70,000 = \underline{\hphantom{0000}}$

15. $6 + 700 + 3,000 + 90,000 + 50 = \underline{\hphantom{0000}}$ **16.** $8 + 300 + 1,000 + 40,000 + 20 = \underline{\hphantom{0000}}$

17. $3,000 + 7 + 50 + 900 + 40,000 = \underline{\hphantom{0000}}$ **18.** $100 + 60 + 10,000 + 4,000 + 1 = \underline{\hphantom{0000}}$

19. $500 + 60 + 90,000 + 3,000 + 4 = \underline{\hphantom{0000}}$ **20.** $7 + 800 + 9,000 + 30,000 + 10 = \underline{\hphantom{0000}}$

Lesson 4

Estimating 1

To estimate a sum or difference, round each number.
Then add or subtract the rounded numbers.

Addition:		Subtraction:	
6 8 8 → 7 0 0		4,0 3 1 → 4,0 0 0	
+ 2 3 1 → + 2 0 0		− 7 8 9 → − 8 0 0	
9 0 0		3,2 0 0	

Estimate and solve the problems below.

1. 8 7 8 → 9 0 0
    + 3 9 1 → + 4 0 0
           1,3 0 0

2. 4 6 1 →
    + 5 4 0 →

3. 1 2 9 →
    + 6 0 7 →

4. 3 9 9 →
    + 7 3 1 →

5. 9 4 3 →
    − 4 9 9 →

6. 7 7 8 →
    − 2 0 7 →

7. 6 3 0 →
    − 4 5 2 →

8. 3 5 6 →
    − 1 7 5 →

Estimating 2

To estimate a sum or difference, round each number. Then add or subtract the rounded numbers.

Estimate and solve the problems below.

1. 6,281 →
 +3,552 →

2. 4,782 →
 +1,321 →

3. 9,423 →
 +6,599 →

4. 5,192 →
 +4,807 →

5. 2,991 →
 +5,841 →

6. 7,510 →
 +7,291 →

7. 1,690 →
 +4,501 →

8. 3,908 →
 +4,687 →

9. 9,499 →
 + 532 →

10. 3,641 →
 - 2,487 →

11. 8,961 →
 - 4,540 →

12. 7,299 →
 - 5,607 →

13. 4,701 →
 - 3,112 →

14. 9,475 →
 - 7,500 →

15. 3,559 →
 - 1,890 →

16. 4,115 →
 - 805 →

17. 5,602 →
 - 2,199 →

18. 7,999 →
 - 5,999 →

Lesson 5

Addition with Regrouping

To add multiple-digit numbers together, start in the ones place and then use basic addition rules. When a number equals ten or more the first digit carries over to the next spot. This is called **regrouping**.

Step 1: Add the digits in the one's column and carry over the 1 to the ten's column.	**Step 2:** Next add the digits in the ten's column and carry over the 1 to the hundred's column.	**Step 3:** Next add the digits in the hundred's column.	**Step 4:** Finally, carry over the 1 from the hundred's column to the thousand's column.
1000's | 100's | 10's | 1's	1000's | 100's | 10's | 1's	1000's | 100's | 10's | 1's	1000's | 100's | 10's | 1's
1	1 1	1 1	1 1
7 | 5 | 9	7 | 5 | 9	7 | 5 | 9	7 | 5 | 9
+ 5 | 6 | 4	+ 5 | 6 | 4	+ 5 | 6 | 4	+ 5 | 6 | 4
[3]	[2] | 3	[3] | 2 | 3	[1] | 3 | 2 | 3

Solve the problems below. Use regrouping when needed.

1. $\begin{array}{r} 944 \\ +281 \\ \hline 1,225 \end{array}$

2. $\begin{array}{r} 603 \\ +421 \\ \hline \end{array}$

3. $\begin{array}{r} 946 \\ +634 \\ \hline \end{array}$

4. $\begin{array}{r} 407 \\ +335 \\ \hline \end{array}$

5. $\begin{array}{r} 289 \\ +972 \\ \hline \end{array}$

6. $\begin{array}{r} 572 \\ +539 \\ \hline \end{array}$

7. $\begin{array}{r} 491 \\ +862 \\ \hline \end{array}$

8. $\begin{array}{r} 945 \\ +687 \\ \hline \end{array}$

9. $\begin{array}{r} 999 \\ +237 \\ \hline \end{array}$

10. $\begin{array}{r} 755 \\ +675 \\ \hline \end{array}$

Lesson 6

4-Digit Addition 1

Solve the problems below using regrouping.

1.	1,091 2,157 + 3,267	**2.**	9,815 803 + 2,216	**3.**	3,891 1,259 + 7,520	**4.**	2,552 8,406 + 271
5.	5,330 1,211 + 9,801	**6.**	4,881 2,009 + 1,987	**7.**	3,072 1,650 + 578	**8.**	1,985 8,105 + 1,776
9.	9,841 2,750 + 1,349	**10.**	5,400 501 + 3,814	**11.**	7,072 6,152 + 1,785	**12.**	707 1,804 + 2,950
13.	2,400 962 + 815	**14.**	6,074 1,255 + 8,079	**15.**	8,180 2,755 + 2,577	**16.**	9,064 9,607 + 6,074
17.	4,911 2,757 + 3,025	**18.**	5,787 6,962 + 1,570	**19.**	7,705 5,321 + 1,766	**20.**	3,033 1,447 + 9,632

4-Digit Addition 2

Solve the problems below using regrouping.

1. 4,982 6,350 9,811 + 2,652	**2.** 5,578 1,669 8,902 + 191	**3.** 2,121 9,279 3,364 + 2,127	**4.** 4,880 6,524 9,967 + 2,115	**5.** 6,159 1,250 1,975 + 9,364
6. 3,160 9,497 5,222 + 4,596	**7.** 6,890 1,457 9,058 + 3,126	**8.** 2,459 9,087 1,134 + 705	**9.** 6,110 993 1,678 + 5,157	**10.** 3,692 1,157 7,239 + 7,058
11. 4,457 9,280 1,170 + 2,357	**12.** 6,898 6,157 3,309 + 675	**13.** 3,070 1,007 4,911 + 7,963	**14.** 5,158 4,058 3,982 + 1,360	**15.** 4,869 6,048 9,263 + 2,009
16. 1,222 1,378 3,157 + 9,009	**17.** 3,089 6,164 7,665 + 5,035	**18.** 2,172 4,339 6,057 + 1,197	**19.** 3,887 3,105 1,007 + 332	**20.** 7,982 3,350 2,811 + 4,652

Lesson 7

5-Digit Addition

Solve the problems below using regrouping.

1. 54,691
    10,847
    + 39,116

2. 90,861
    77,392
    + 20,691

3. 44,388
    35,512
    + 64,172

4. 50,233
    46,397
    + 92,846

5. 58,732
    33,020
    + 12,571

6. 19,570
    27,694
    + 56,630

7. 90,691
    51,072
    + 14,321

8. 35,450
    82,300
    + 23,124

9. 60,805
    84,997
    + 39,111

10. 66,349
    70,244
    + 11,188

11. 15,000
    39,289
    + 2,723

12. 99,785
    35,562
    + 48,078

13. 38,058
    36,298
    + 57,613

14. 66,951
    23,207
    + 10,881

15. 47,381
    61,273
    + 75,507

16. 94,080
    11,636
    + 9,860

17. 39,005
    29,678
    + 14,567

18. 48,399
    15,467
    + 5,005

19. 18,222
    90,309
    + 66,009

20. 99,863
    99,067
    + 65,331

Lesson 8

6-Digit Addition

Solve the problems below using regrouping.

1. 102,220
    366,357
    + 127,475

2. 557,365
    166,204
    + 254,129

3. 325,299
    770,351
    + 64,658

4. 129,195
    632,744
    + 335,163

5. 641,001
    237,925
    + 210,137

6. 752,112
    209,482
    + 322,165

7. 480,129
    638,635
    + 218,001

8. 500,051
    217,521
    + 127,937

9. 637,817
    289,364
    + 123,994

10. 491,065
    278,605
    + 316,221

11. 841,316
    958,375
    + 175,363

12. 150,633
    534,110
    + 156,925

13. 655,119
    230,754
    + 524,239

14. 163,159
    952,364
    + 402,846

15. 752,005
    647,119
    + 841,715

16. 363,175
    119,376
    + 237,860

17. 445,123
    967,525
    + 364,129

18. 638,117
    500,682
    + 438,385

19. 781,975
    237,105
    + 285,367

20. 908,129
    117,765
    + 637,032

Lesson 9

7-Digit Addition

 Solve the problems below using regrouping.

1. 3,541,277 6,129,245 + 2,382,107	2. 2,711,015 3,844,362 + 1,332,745	3. 5,008,694 3,992,406 + 8,264,367	4. 8,267,200 7,164,245 + 6,277,594
5. 5,466,999 3,050,638 + 6,105,347	6. 7,548,007 2,215,635 + 1,365,815	7. 9,147,129 6,308,905 + 4,315,707	8. 5,113,799 5,564,002 + 6,465,355
9. 1,648,912 3,154,099 + 5,367,474	10. 6,905,011 4,322,966 + 3,375,378	11. 6,475,619 9,504,242 + 7,289,071	12. 1,299,151 3,637,889 + 8,652,234
13. 3,552,910 7,313,577 + 4,429,964	14. 6,008,799 5,027,346 + 6,244,310	15. 1,224,799 1,496,843 + 9,841,000	16. 4,208,577 5,995,685 + 5,372,129
17. 6,141,654 1,764,889 + 7,633,924	18. 5,639,047 6,129,885 + 3,445,369	19. 9,665,007 8,682,420 + 4,341,204	20. 5,245,895 6,636,635 + 8,547,118

Lesson 10

Subtraction with Borrowing

To subtract and borrow, start with the ones column. If the bottom number is of a greater value, you have to borrow from the next column.

Step 1:	Step 2:	Step 3:	Step 4:
Any time the bottom number in a column is of greater value than the top number, you need to borrow.	Borrow 10 from the next column. This reduces the 6 to 5 and increases the number in the first column from 3 to 13.	Now we need to borrow 10 from the hundreds column. This reduces the 7 to 6 and increases the numbers in the tens column from 5 to 15.	Now you are ready for the final step. Finish by subtracting the numbers in all the columns.

Step 1:
```
100's 10's 1's
  7    6    3
- 4    8    5
```

Step 2:
```
100's 10's 1's
            5
  7    6   13
- 4    8    5
```

Step 3:
```
100's 10's 1's
   6   15
  7    6   13
- 4    8    5
```

Step 4:
```
100's 10's 1's
   6   15
  7    6   13
- 4    8    5
   2    7    8
```

Use borrowing to solve the problems below.

1. 682
  − 239
  ‾‾‾‾‾
    443

2. 909
  − 457

3. 342
  − 199

4. 511
  − 227

5. 704
  − 165

6. 467
  − 349

7. 919
  − 58

8. 609
  − 158

9. 711
  − 459

10. 197
  − 68

11. 679
  − 388

12. 537
  − 87

13. 892
  − 604

14. 906
  − 449

15. 637
  − 205

Lesson 11

4-Digit Subtraction

 Use what you learned about borrowing to solve the problems below.

1. 6,432
   − 5,320

2. 2,675
   − 1,564

3. 4,233
   − 452

4. 5,428
   − 2,649

5. 1,995
   − 239

6. 7,321
   − 834

7. 9,211
   − 1,700

8. 3,946
   − 1,682

9. 2,463
   − 1,939

10. 8,959
    − 3,274

11. 1,295
    − 968

12. 9,942
    − 7,895

13. 7,542
    − 2,907

14. 3,649
    − 1,590

15. 9,864
    − 4,389

16. 3,888
    − 999

17. 5,001
    − 3,547

18. 1,775
    − 859

19. 3,880
    − 1,125

20. 9,567
    − 6,820

Lesson 12

5-Digit Subtraction

Use what you learned about borrowing to solve the problems below.

1. 25,911 − 23,125	**2.** 40,127 − 15,089	**3.** 68,956 − 47,580	**4.** 42,207 − 5,699
5. 30,113 − 9,357	**6.** 92,253 − 75,449	**7.** 57,115 − 36,608	**8.** 21,659 − 17,102
9. 81,678 − 44,169	**10.** 47,827 − 9,018	**11.** 35,157 − 16,658	**12.** 50,011 − 23,956
13. 29,368 − 13,504	**14.** 48,638 − 5,174	**15.** 59,239 − 14,107	**16.** 66,250 − 20,078
17. 36,754 − 18,265	**18.** 54,587 − 33,058	**19.** 63,017 − 5,582	**20.** 92,236 − 15,297

Lesson 13

6-Digit Subtraction

 Use what you learned about borrowing to solve the problems below.

1. 627,343
    − 495,861

2. 854,115
    − 346,264

3. 506,925
    − 229,167

4. 129,239
    − 95,226

5. 958,062
    − 179,687

6. 297,343
    − 105,907

7. 961,343
    − 550,097

8. 639,447
    − 287,334

9. 339,081
    − 117,118

10. 520,142
    − 287,963

11. 728,253
    − 681,175

12. 550,008
    − 368,764

13. 785,780
    − 358,999

14. 902,144
    − 751,100

15. 811,654
    − 436,907

16. 495,861
    − 399,000

17. 447,675
    − 258,007

18. 781,115
    − 369,098

19. 265,017
    − 65,336

20. 965,305
    − 345,999

Lesson 14

7-Digit Subtraction

Use what you learned about borrowing to
solve the problems below.

1. 2,135,209
    − 1,542,921

2. 4,275,394
    − 2,866,100

3. 6,429,925
    −   699,295

4. 5,985,324
    − 3,547,935

5. 7,122,956
    − 5,009,122

6. 5,588,133
    −   367,794

7. 9,002,357
    − 1,688,188

8. 8,652,116
    − 5,775,209

9. 6,339,100
    − 3,203,548

10. 9,000,142
    − 3,872,482

11. 7,125,951
    − 5,324,007

12. 5,689,008
    − 1,005,956

13. 9,958,111
    − 6,832,504

14. 7,194,926
    − 2,607,299

15. 4,305,842
    −   635,184

16. 8,965,122
    − 5,594,009

17. 6,487,070
    −   8,199

18. 9,488,267
    − 7,129,098

19. 6,125,199
    − 2.658,037

20. 5,600,204
    − 3,317,869

Lesson 15

8-Digit Subtraction

Use what you learned about borrowing to solve the problems below.

1. 32,445,311
    − 19,306,805

2. 54,009,812
    − 23,329,605

3. 72,511,420
    − 49,964,122

4. 43,652,019
    − 7,994,364

5. 17,457,333
    − 9,864,127

6. 85,674,152
    − 39,200,997

7. 55,925,321
    −   365,544

8. 90,899,425
    − 1,621,678

9. 69,129,364
    − 34,330,657

10. 84,994,657
    − 65,732,566

11. 88,299,882
    − 2,164,295

12. 39,599,635
    − 10,124,988

13. 67,290,975
    − 2,364,963

14. 50,400,991
    − 6,536,027

15. 42,633,635
    − 12,396,864

16. 95,155,964
    − 57,377,337

17. 82,112,650
    −   820,941

18. 75,644,340
    − 38,637,652

19. 59,965,122
    − 3,637,569

20. 93,050,002
    − 54,864,632

21. 66,965,362
    −   167,064

22. 92,338,674
    − 17,211,995

23. 44,294,632
    − 29,009,367

24. 84,962,366
    − 52,507,999

Chapter 2 - Multiplication and Exponents

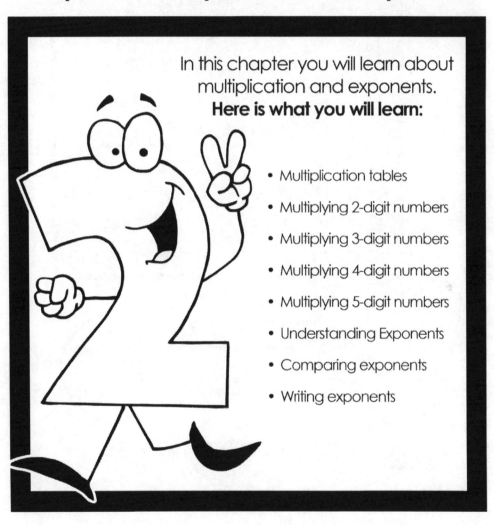

Chapter 2 - Multiplication and Exponents

In this chapter you will learn about multiplication and exponents.
Here is what you will learn:

- Multiplication tables
- Multiplying 2-digit numbers
- Multiplying 3-digit numbers
- Multiplying 4-digit numbers
- Multiplying 5-digit numbers
- Understanding Exponents
- Comparing exponents
- Writing exponents

Multiplication Table

x	1	2	3	4	5	6	7	8	9	10
1	1	2	3	4	5	6	7	8	9	10
2	2	4	6	8	10	12	14	16	18	20
3	3	6	9	12	15	18	21	24	27	30
4	4	8	12	16	20	24	28	32	36	40
5	5	10	15	20	25	30	35	40	45	50
6	6	12	18	24	30	36	42	48	54	60
7	7	14	21	28	35	42	49	56	63	70
8	8	16	24	32	40	48	56	64	72	80
9	9	18	27	36	45	54	63	72	81	90
10	10	20	30	40	50	60	70	80	90	100

This is a **multiplication table**.
It shows how numbers multiply together.
The numbers in the **top row** multiply
by the numbers in the **left side row**.
Match up the rows to get your answer.

Lesson 1

Blank Multiplication Table

This is a multiplication table. Multiply the numbers in the top row by the numbers in the side row to get the product.

X	1	2	3	4	5	6	7	8	9	10
1										
2										
3										
4										
5										
6										
7										
8										
9										
10										

Multiplication Table Mix-up

X	1	2	3
1	1	2	3
2	2	4	6

This is a multiplication table. Multiply the numbers in the top row by the numbers in the side row to get the product.

1.

X	4	5	6
6			
5			
4			
3			
2			

2.

X	0	6	8	4	9
5					
4					
3					

3.

X	2	3	4	5	6
10					
11					
12					

4.

X	5	4	3
6			
5			
4			
3			
2			

Lesson 2

Multiplication

To multiply a one-digit number by a two-digit number with regrouping, start in the ones place and then use basic multiplication rules. When the number equals ten or more the first digit carries over to the next spot. This is called **regrouping**.

	Hundreds	Tens	Ones
Step 1: Multiply the numbers in the ones column and carry the first digit over to the tens column.	2	4	7
	x		3
			1

$3 \times 7 = 21$

	Hundreds	Tens	Ones
Step 2: Multiply the digit in at the bottom of the ones column by the digit in the tens column and add the regrouped number.	2 + 4		7
	x		3
		4	1

$4 \times 3 = 12$ Then $12 + 2 = 14$

	Hundreds	Tens	Ones
Step 3: The one then carries over to the hundreds place.	2	4	7
	x		3
	1	4	1

Answer $= 141$

Solve the problems below.

1. 6 5
    x   4
    ———
    2 6 0

2. 4 9
    x   3
    ———

3. 1 2
    x   9
    ———

4. 9 2
    x   6
    ———

5. 5 7
    x   8
    ———

6. 4 9
    x   8
    ———

7. 2 9
    x   4
    ———

8. 3 2
    x   5
    ———

9. 6 8
    x   7
    ———

10. 8 3
    x   9
    ———

Lesson 3

Multiplication by 2-Digit Numbers

To multiply a two-digit number by a two-digit number, start in the ones place and then use basic multiplication and addition rules. Don't forget to use what you've learned about regrouping.

1. Multiply by the **ones** multiplier.	2. Multiply by the **tens** multiplier.	3. Add the products.
Hundreds | Tens | Ones	Hundreds | Tens | Ones	Hundreds | Tens | Ones
2 + 4 6 x 2 4 1 8 4	1 + 4 6 x 2 4 1 8 4 + 9 2 0	4 6 x 2 4 1 8 4 + 9 2 0 1 1 0 4
4 is the first multiplier 4 x 46 = 184	**20 is the second multiplier** 20 x 46 = 104	**Add the two products** 184 + 920 = 1,104

Solve the problems below.

1.
```
     8 2
   x 2 4
   ─────
     3 2 8
 + 1 6 4 0
 ─────────
   1,9 6 8
```

2.
```
    9 9
  x 3 2
  ─────
```

3.
```
    2 7
  x 1 6
  ─────
```

4.
```
    5 4
  x 3 6
  ─────
```

5.
```
    7 2
  x 2 9
  ─────
```

6.
```
    3 7
  x 2 8
  ─────
```

7.
```
    5 5
  x 1 7
  ─────
```

8.
```
    6 2
  x 3 3
  ─────
```

9.
```
    9 2
  x 1 8
  ─────
```

10.
```
    2 4
  x 1 2
  ─────
```

- 34 -

Lesson 4

Multiplying 2-Digit Numbers by 2-Digit Numbers

To multiply a two-digit number by a two-digit number, start in the ones place and then use basic multiplication and addition rules. Dont forget to use what you've learned about regrouping.

Solve the problems below.

1. 49 x 1 5	**2.** 64 x 2 4	**3.** 54 x 3 6	**4.** 67 x 4 8	**5.** 85 x 6 5
6. 74 x 4 6	**7.** 86 x 3 9	**8.** 35 x 2 9	**9.** 68 x 4 7	**10.** 72 x 2 5
11. 54 x 5 4	**12.** 87 x 6 4	**13.** 62 x 4 3	**14.** 95 x 9 2	**15.** 42 x 3 9
16. 96 x 7 5	**17.** 84 x 1 5	**18.** 98 x 6 7	**19.** 76 x 2 8	**20.** 65 x 5 7

Lesson 5

Multiplication Word Problems

Use multiplication to solve the problems below.

1. If Tommy plays 7 soccer games, and he blocks 6 shots in each game, how many shots will he block?

2. Larry loves photography and takes a lot of pictures. If he takes 32 pictures a day for 20 days, how many pictures will he take?

3. James is a great painter. He can paint 3 paintings a day. If he paints for 19 days how many paintings will he have?

4. Brian eats pizza every day. If he eats 8 slices a day for 9 days how many slices of pizza will he eat?

Lesson 6

Multiplying 3-Digit Numbers by 2-Digit Numbers 1

To multiply a three-digit number by a two-digit number, start in the ones place and then use basic multiplication and addition rules. Dont forget to use what you've learned about regrouping.

Solve the problems below.

1. 3 2 1
    x 2 3
    -----
    9 6 3
    + 6 4 2 0

    7,3 8 3

2. 2 5 9
    x 1 9

3. 5 1 2
    x 4 3

4. 4 5 9
    x 3 6

5. 6 0 8
    x 2 5

6. 6 4 1
    x 3 9

7. 5 3 9
    x 6 2

8. 2 3 5
    x 2 4

9. 6 8 4
    x 3 1

10. 8 4 3
    x 6 4

11. 8 9 2
    x 8 3

12. 3 9 9
    x 9 5

13. 7 0 5
    x 3 4

14. 6 3 3
    x 7 9

15. 5 1 4
    x 9 2

16. 4 5 5
    x 9 9

17. 9 5 0
    x 6 4

18. 6 9 6
    x 8 2

19. 7 8 9
    x 3 4

20. 8 6 5
    x 9 6

Multiplying 3-Digit Numbers by 2-Digit Numbers 2

To multiply a three-digit number by a two-digit number, start in the ones place and then use basic multiplication and addition rules. Dont forget to use what you've learned about regrouping.

Solve the problems below.

1. 4 9 1
    x 5 2

2. 9 0 3
    x 3 2

3. 3 8 4
    x 9 4

4. 6 8 9
    x 1 7

5. 7 3 2
    x 5 7

6. 5 5 9
    x 7 3

7. 1 9 7
    x 4 4

8. 2 9 4
    x 5 4

9. 3 1 6
    x 2 9

10. 9 1 7
    x 3 4

11. 8 2 7
    x 1 2

12. 4 9 4
    x 3 7

13. 6 5 9
    x 9 6

14. 7 4 9
    x 6 1

15. 5 2 7
    x 7 2

16. 3 9 9
    x 5 7

17. 8 9 9
    x 7 5

18. 4 2 1
    x 3 4

19. 6 2 5
    x 8 4

20. 9 6 4
    x 6 6

Lesson 7

Multiplication Word Problems 2

Use multiplication to solve the problems below.

1. George has lots of pigs. He keeps 147 pigs in each pen. He has 23 pens. How many pigs does he have in all?

2. Penny is cooking muffins. She can cook 4 muffins per pan. She has 239 pans. How many muffins can she cook?

3. Mickey is going trick or treating. If he goes to 128 houses and collects 12 pieces of candy at each house, how much candy will Mickey have?

4. Nathan is a talented basketball player. If he scores 19 points in each of his next 32 games, how many points will he score?

Lesson 8

Multiplying 4-Digit Numbers by 2-Digit Numbers 1

To multiply a four-digit number by a two-digit number, start in the ones place and then use basic multiplication and addition rules. Don't forget to use what you've learned about regrouping.

Solve the problems below.

1. 1,491
   x   52
   ——————
     2982
   + 74550
   ——————
   77,532

2. 6,861
   x   15

3. 4,532
   x   37

4. 2,725
   x   93

5. 3,116
   x   29

6. 7,683
   x   49

7. 4,492
   x   66

8. 2,374
   x   97

9. 5,051
   x   31

10. 8,790
    x   29

11. 2,778
    x   86

12. 6,627
    x   61

13. 3,055
    x   57

14. 6,812
    x   89

15. 4,558
    x   64

16. 5,109
    x   51

17. 9,582
    x   75

18. 7,716
    x   68

19. 3,337
    x   35

20. 8,274
    x   59

Multiplying 4-Digit Numbers by 2-Digit Numbers 2

To multiply a four-digit number by a two-digit number, start in the ones place and then use basic multiplication and addition rules. Don't forget to use what you've learned about regrouping.

Solve the problems below.

1. 2,631
   x 12

2. 3,437
   x 20

3. 6,115
   x 25

4. 1,037
   x 31

5. 4,624
   x 29

6. 5,297
   x 33

7. 1,608
   x 37

8. 4,809
   x 47

9. 5,194
   x 10

10. 3,578
    x 36

11. 8,167
    x 57

12. 5,802
    x 66

13. 4,950
    x 42

14. 9,568
    x 67

15. 7,827
    x 74

16. 9,972
    x 27

17. 5,302
    x 37

18. 8,185
    x 97

19. 6,375
    x 88

20. 9,219
    x 96

Lesson 9

Multiplying 3-Digit Numbers by 3-Digit Numbers 1

To multiply a three-digit number by a three-digit number, start in the ones place and then use basic multiplication and addition rules. Don't forget to use what you've learned about regrouping.

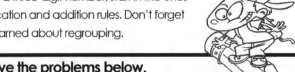

Solve the problems below.

1.
```
     4 3 2
   x 3 6 5
   ───────
     2,1 6 0
    2 5,9 2 0
 + 1 2 9,6 0 0
 ───────────
   1 5 7,6 8 0
```

2.
```
     3 5 9
   x 6 1 9
```

3.
```
     4 8 2
   x 1 6 5
```

4.
```
     7 4 2
   x 3 6 3
```

5.
```
     4 7 6
   x 1 3 4
```

6.
```
     8 9 5
   x 1 3 5
```

7.
```
     9 2 2
   x 6 1 7
```

8.
```
     3 8 4
   x 4 7 5
```

9.
```
     5 2 4
   x 2 7 7
```

10.
```
     9 1 5
   x 6 7 4
```

11.
```
     5 9 5
   x 1 8 6
```

12.
```
     8 0 7
   x 1 3 2
```

13.
```
     9 1 5
   x 3 3 7
```

14.
```
     9 3 5
   x 4 7 6
```

15.
```
     4 8 2
   x 9 8 2
```

Multiplying 3-Digit Numbers by 3-Digit Numbers 2

To multiply a three-digit number by a three-digit number, start in the ones place and then use basic multiplication and addition rules. Don't forget to use what you've learned about regrouping.

Solve the problems below.

1. 367
    x 182

2. 227
    x 307

3. 521
    x 497

4. 139
    x 927

5. 865
    x 267

6. 556
    x 234

7. 682
    x 264

8. 905
    x 114

9. 946
    x 371

10. 568
    x 436

11. 637
    x 220

12. 274
    x 369

13. 857
    x 237

14. 475
    x 602

15. 552
    x 189

16. 648
    x 422

17. 592
    x 305

18. 200
    x 967

19. 637
    x 137

20. 659
    x 884

Lesson 10

Multiplying 4-Digit Numbers by 3-Digit Numbers 1

To multiply a four-digit number by a three-digit number, start in the ones place and then use basic multiplication and addition rules. Don't forget to use what you've learned about regrouping.

Solve the problems below.

1. 1,291
   x 324

   5164
   25820
   +387300

   418,284

2. 2,177
   x 115

3. 4,264
   x 137

4. 3,387
   x 244

5. 5,189
   x 320

6. 3,654
   x 439

7. 5,307
   x 148

8. 2,273
   x 259

9. 4,892
   x 341

10. 5,952
    x 326

11. 6,489
    x 566

12. 2,701
    x 424

13. 3,119
    x 178

14. 5,297
    x 626

15. 9,436
    x 339

16. 3,624
    x 749

17. 7,117
    x 572

18. 5,930
    x 897

19. 8,175
    x 688

20. 6,408
    x 960

Multiplying 4-Digit Numbers by 3-Digit Numbers 2

To multiply a four-digit number by a three-digit number, start in the ones place and then use basic multiplication and addition rules. Don't forget to use what you've learned about regrouping.

Solve the problems below.

1. 6,584
   x 324

2. 3,291
   x 105

3. 8,347
   x 137

4. 4,551
   x 244

5. 9,067
   x 320

6. 6,561
   x 439

7. 7,812
   x 140

8. 3,302
   x 259

9. 5,191
   x 341

10. 4,073
    x 326

11. 8,651
    x 560

12. 3,291
    x 424

13. 5,067
    x 682

14. 5,297
    x 119

15. 9,436
    x 207

16. 3,624
    x 329

17. 7,117
    x 708

18. 5,930
    x 132

19. 8,175
    x 985

20. 6,408
    x 560

Lesson 11

Exponents 1

An **exponent** is a number that tells how many times the base is used as a factor. It is written as a smaller number placed above and to the right of the base number.

Example:	Example:
$5^3 = 125$	$3^4 = 81$
$(5 \times 5 \times 5) = 125$	$(3 \times 3 \times 3 \times 3) = 81$
5 is the base number and 3 is the exponent	3 is the base number and 4 is the exponent

Write the exponents for each set of numbers.

1. $6 \times 6 \times 6 \times 6$ = $\underline{6^4}$

2. $3 \times 3 \times 3$ = _____

3. $5 \times 5 \times 5$ = _____

4. $7 \times 7 \times 7 \times 7$ = _____

5. $9 \times 9 \times 9 \times 9 \times 9$ = _____

6. $8 \times 8 \times 8 \times 8 \times 8 \times 8$ = _____

7. $2 \times 2 \times 2 \times 2 \times 2 \times 2$ = _____

8. $4 \times 4 \times 4 \times 4$ = _____

9. $5 \times 5 \times 5$ = _____

10. $6 \times 6 \times 6 \times 6 \times 6$ = _____

11. $7 \times 7 \times 7 \times 7 \times 7 \times 7 \times 7$ = _____

12. $2 \times 2 \times 2$ = _____

13. $3 \times 3 \times 3 \times 3$ = _____

14. $9 \times 9 \times 9 \times 9 \times 9 \times 9$ = _____

Lesson 12

Exponents 2

Write out the exponents below and solve. Use the boxes to work out the problems,

---

1. 9^3 = _____ 9 x 9 x 9 _____ = 729   **2.** 5^5 = _____ = ___

3. 8^4 = _____ = ___   **4.** 2^9 = _____ = ___

5. 6^4 = _____ = ___   **6.** 4^5 = _____ = ___

Lesson 13

Exponents 3

Write out the exponents below and solve. Use the boxes to work out the problems,

---

1. $8^2 =$ _____ = _____

2. $6^5 =$ _____ = _____

3. $7^4 =$ _____ = _____

4. $3^8 =$ _____ = _____

5. $4^3 =$ _____ = _____

6. $5^5 =$ _____ = _____

Comparing Exponents

An **exponent** is a number that tells how many times the base is used as a factor. It is written as a smaller number placed above and to the right of the base number.

Fill in the blanks to answer if each set is greater than, less than or equal.

1. 3^2 $\boxed{<}$ 2^4

2. 4^3 $\square$ 3^2

3. 2^4 $\square$ 5^2

4. 6^5 $\square$ 4^3

5. 3^3 $\square$ 5^2

6. 5^3 $\square$ 7^2

7. 8^4 $\square$ 5^3

8. 6^3 $\square$ 9^3

9. 4^4 $\square$ 8^4

10. 5^2 $\square$ 9^2

11. 7^3 $\square$ 2^2

12. 4^4 $\square$ 3^2

13. 8^3 $\square$ 4^2

14. 3^4 $\square$ 9^3

15. 6^2 $\square$ 7^2

Chapter 3 - Division

In this chapter you will learn about division of large numbers.
Here are the things you will learn:

- Understanding Division

- Division with Remainders

- Division of 2-digit numbers

- Division of 3-digit numbers

- Division of 4-digit numbers

- Division of 5-digit numbers

Division

- Division is a way to find out how many times one number is counted in another number.

- The ÷ sign means "divided by".

- Use this symbol $\overline{)}$ to set up a division problem.

- The dividend is the larger number that is divided by the smaller number, the divisor.

- The answer of a division problem is called the quotient.

÷ is the symbol for division

$$6 \div 2 = 3$$

dividend   divisor   quotient

- $6 \div 2 = 3$ is read "6 divided by 2 is equal to 3".

- In $6 \div 2 = 3$, the divisor is 2, the dividend is 6 and the quotient is 3.

$\overline{)}$ is used to divide

$$2\overline{)10}^{5}$$

divisor   dividend   quotient

- $2\overline{)10}\,^{5}$ is read "10 divided by 2 is equal to 5".

- In $2\overline{)10}\,^{5}$, the divisor is 2, the dividend is 10 and the quotient is 5.

Lesson 1

Division with a 2-Digit Dividend 1

When dividing a **two-digit number** by a **one-digit number**, the quotient can have one or two digits. That is why it is easier to start by breaking the problem down into steps.

Estimate	Divide the tens	Bring down the ones and repeat the steps.	The answer is: **28 r 1**
$\dfrac{2}{3\overline{)85}}$	$\begin{array}{r} 2 \\ 3\overline{)85} \\ -6 \\ \hline 2 \end{array}$	$\begin{array}{r} 28 \\ 3\overline{)85} \\ -6\!\downarrow \\ \hline 25 \\ -24 \\ \hline 1 \end{array}$	Remember these steps:
Take a look at the first digit. Estimate how many times 3 will go into 8 without going over the number.	3 can go into 8 twice. Multiply 3 x 2 and get 6. Subtract the 6 from 8 leaving 2.	Bring down the 5 from the one's column and repeat the steps. **The remainder is 1**	1. Divide 2. Multiply 3. Subtract 4. Bring down Repeat these steps until there are no more digits to bring down.

Solve these problems. Some may not have remainders.

1.
$$\begin{array}{r} 16\,r1 \\ 6\overline{)97} \\ -6 \\ \hline 37 \\ -36 \\ \hline 1 \end{array}$$

2. $5\overline{)38}$

3. $7\overline{)89}$

4. $2\overline{)91}$

4. $4\overline{)99}$

6. $3\overline{)44}$

7. $5\overline{)58}$

8. $2\overline{)67}$

Lesson 2

Division with a 2-Digit Dividend 2

 Solve these problems. Some may not have remainders.

1. 5)67   2. 8)99   3. 3)53   4. 9)92

5. 2)78   6. 7)80   7. 5)73   8. 3)64

9. 4)61   10. 2)83   11. 9)97   12. 6)77

Lesson 3

Division Word Problems

Use division to solve the problems below.

1. Jerry has 24 boxes to move. He can only carry 3 boxes at a time. How many trips will he have to make to move all the boxes?

2. Sandy has 15 chores to do around the house this week. If she does 3 chores a day, how many days will it take her to do all her chores?

3. Mitchell has 42 apples. He wants to divide them into 6 groups. How many apples will be in each group?

4. Andy has 63 cookies in his jar that he wants to share with his friends. If he has 7 friends, how many cookies will each friend get?

Lesson 4

Dividing 3-Digit Dividends by a 1-Digit Divisor 1

When dividing a larger number by a one-digit number, it is easier to start by breaking the problem down into steps.

Always remember these steps

1. Estimate
2. Divide
3. Multiply
4. Subtract
5. Compare
6. Bring down

Repeat the steps as needed

Here is an example:

Estimate	Divide the hundreds	Bring down the tens and repeat the steps.	Bring down the ones and repeat the steps.
$$\begin{array}{r} 2 \\ 4\overline{)975} \end{array}$$	$$\begin{array}{r} 2 \\ 4\overline{)975} \\ -8 \\ \hline 1 \end{array}$$	$$\begin{array}{r} 24 \\ 4\overline{)975} \\ -8\downarrow \\ \hline 17 \\ -16 \\ \hline 1 \end{array}$$	$$\begin{array}{r} 243r3 \\ 4\overline{)975} \\ -8 \\ \hline 17 \\ -16\downarrow \\ \hline 15 \\ -12 \\ \hline 3 \end{array}$$
Take a look at the first digit. Estimate how many times 4 will go into 9 without going over the number.	4 can go into 9 twice. Multiply 4 x 2 and get 8. Subtract the 8 from 9 leaving 1.	4 can go into 17 four times. Multiply 4 x 4 and get 16. Subtract 16 from 17 leaving 1.	The remainder is **3**

Solve these problems. Some may not have remainders.

1.
$$\begin{array}{r} 367\,r\,1 \\ 2\overline{)735} \\ -6 \\ \hline 13 \\ -12 \\ \hline 15 \\ -14 \\ \hline 1 \end{array}$$

2. $3\overline{)892}$

3. $7\overline{)938}$

Lesson 5

Dividing 3-Digit Dividends by a 1-Digit Divisor 2

Solve these problems. Some may not have remainders.

1.
```
    153r2
3)461
  -3
  ‾‾
   16
  -15
  ‾‾‾
    11
   -9
   ‾‾
    2
```

2. 4)128

3. 2)392

4. 7)975

5. 9)815

6. 6)892

7. 3)564

8. 2)297

9. 3)622

10. 4)930

11. 5)556

12. 7)986

13. 2)846

14. 3)134

15. 2)408

16. 2)276

17. 3)578

18. 8)556

19. 9)681

20. 4)599

Dividing 3-Digit Dividends by a 1-Digit Divisor 3

 Solve these problems. Some may not have remainders.

1. 9)592   2. 5)344   3. 7)907   4. 2)677   5. 6)128

6. 3)750   7. 4)417   8. 8)982   9. 9)337   10. 3)827

11. 6)679   12. 2)736   13. 5)422   14. 7)175   15. 8)697

16. 9)858   17. 2)907   18. 4)335   19. 9)875   20. 5)785

- 57 -

Lesson 6

Dividing 4-Digit Dividends by a 1-Digit Divisor

Solve these problems. Some may not have remainders.

1. $5\overline{)6,207}$

2. $8\overline{)4,557}$

3. $2\overline{)3,045}$

4. $9\overline{)5,671}$

5. $7\overline{)9,278}$

6. $4\overline{)8,715}$

7. $3\overline{)1,896}$

8. $6\overline{)5,809}$

9. $5\overline{)2,254}$

10. $2\overline{)3,735}$

11. $6\overline{)6,854}$

12. $9\overline{)8,994}$

Lesson 7

Dividing 5-Digit Dividends by a 1-Digit Divisor 1

Solve these problems. Some may not have remainders.

1.
```
        8,447 r3
   4)33,791
    -32
      17
     -16
      19
     -16
      31
     -28
       3
```

2. 3)64,872

3. 6)43,951

4. 2)89,305

5. 7)51,372

6. 5)90,139

7. 9)81,225

8. 3)54,981

9. 4)78,241

10. 7)28,356

11. 6)99,807

12. 9)70,207

- 59 -

Dividing 5-Digit Dividends by 1-Digit Divisor 2

 Solve these problems. Some may not have remainders.

1. $9\overline{)40,863}$

2. $6\overline{)92,025}$

3. $8\overline{)17,283}$

4. $7\overline{)59,518}$

5. $2\overline{)64,761}$

6. $5\overline{)51,909}$

7. $3\overline{)73,871}$

8. $8\overline{)81,095}$

9. $6\overline{)79,812}$

10. $4\overline{)33,299}$

11. $9\overline{)30,956}$

12. $7\overline{)99,068}$

Lesson 8

Division Word Problems 2

Use division to solve the problems below.

1. Reggie has 312 letters to deliver. If he delivers 6 letters an hour, how many hours will it take him to deliver all the letters?

2. Suzy is running a marathon. She needs to run 286 miles to finish. She can run 22 miles a day. How many days will it take her to finish the marathon?

3. Ray has 714 square feet of snow to shovel from his yard. He can shovel 14 square feet an hour. How many hours will it take him to shovel all the snow?

4. Dad is building a fence. He has 595 boards. It takes 5 boards to build each section of the fence. How many sections of fence can he make with the boards he has?

Lesson 9

Division with 2-Digit Divisors

When dividing a larger number by a two-digit number, it is easier to start by breaking the problem down into steps.

Always remember these steps

1. Estimate
2. Divide
3. Multiply
4. Subtract
5. Compare
6. Bring down

Repeat the steps as needed

Here is an example:

Estimate	Divide the first set.	Bring down the ones and repeat the steps.	Bring the remainder back up top.
$$\begin{array}{r} 3 \\ 24\overline{)865} \end{array}$$	$$\begin{array}{r} 3 \\ 24\overline{)865} \\ -72 \\ \hline 14 \end{array}$$	$$\begin{array}{r} 36 \\ 24\overline{)865} \\ -72\downarrow \\ \hline 145 \\ -144 \\ \hline 1 \end{array}$$	$$\begin{array}{r} 36\,r\,1 \\ 24\overline{)865} \\ -72\downarrow \\ \hline 145 \\ -144 \\ \hline 1 \end{array}$$
Take a look at the first digits. Estimate how many times 24 will go into 86 without going over the number.	24 can go into 86 three times equaling 72. Subtract 72 from 86 leaving 14.	24 can go into 145 six times giving us 144. Subtract 144 from 145 leaving 1.	The remainder is 1

Solve these problems. Some may not have remainders.

1. $$\begin{array}{r} 21\,r\,8 \\ 31\overline{)659} \\ -62 \\ \hline 39 \\ -31 \\ \hline 8 \end{array}$$

2. $46\overline{)884}$

3. $21\overline{)429}$

4. $19\overline{)708}$

5. $38\overline{)594}$

6. $75\overline{)999}$

7. $53\overline{)864}$

8. $60\overline{)729}$

9. $91\overline{)963}$

10. $43\overline{)836}$

Lesson 10

Dividing 3-Digit Dividends by a 2-Digit Divisor

 Solve these problems. Some may not have remainders.

1.
$$\begin{array}{r} 22\,r5 \\ 12\overline{)269} \\ -24 \\ \hline 29 \\ -24 \\ \hline 5 \end{array}$$

2. $30\overline{)738}$

3. $22\overline{)449}$

4. $41\overline{)209}$

5. $20\overline{)861}$

6. $12\overline{)271}$

7. $45\overline{)994}$

8. $33\overline{)735}$

9. $35\overline{)755}$

10. $11\overline{)195}$

11. $29\overline{)312}$

12. $63\overline{)656}$

13. $24\overline{)681}$

14. $15\overline{)575}$

15. $20\overline{)468}$

16. $41\overline{)630}$

17. $43\overline{)129}$

18. $39\overline{)705}$

19. $51\overline{)362}$

20. $67\overline{)197}$

- 63 -

Lesson 11

Dividing 4-Digit Dividends by a 2-Digit Divisor

 Solve these problems. Some may not have remainders.

1. $13\overline{)2,691}$ 2. $24\overline{)3,558}$ 3. $65\overline{)8,945}$

4. $54\overline{)6,021}$ 5. $41\overline{)9,278}$ 6. $23\overline{)5,968}$

7. $36\overline{)7,682}$ 8. $17\overline{)4,950}$ 9. $44\overline{)8,962}$

10. $16\overline{)1,891}$ 11. $21\overline{)3,398}$ 12. $32\overline{)6,570}$

Lesson 12

Dividing 5-Digit Dividends by a 2-Digit Divisor 1

 Solve these problems. Some may not have remainders.

```
       3,229 r8
1. 12)38,756
     -36
       27
      -24
        35
       -24
        116
       -108
          8
```

2. 34)85,097

3. 57)96,134

4. 29)64,893

5. 45)95,507

6. 61)35,692

7. 32)96,599

8. 43)77,039

9. 59)32,072

10. 86)90,965

11. 71)80,099

12. 27)43,992

- 65 -

Dividing 5-Digit Dividends by a 2-Digit Divisor 2

 Solve these problems. Some may not have remainders.

1. 29)66,126　　**2.** 18)40,834　　**3.** 43)54,957　　**4.** 36)37,993

5. 56)76,013　　**6.** 84)99,957　　**7.** 70)32,142　　**8.** 33)33,962

9. 44)59,195　　**10.** 91)85,809　　**11.** 62)65,135　　**12.** 89)99,066

Chapter 4 - Fractions

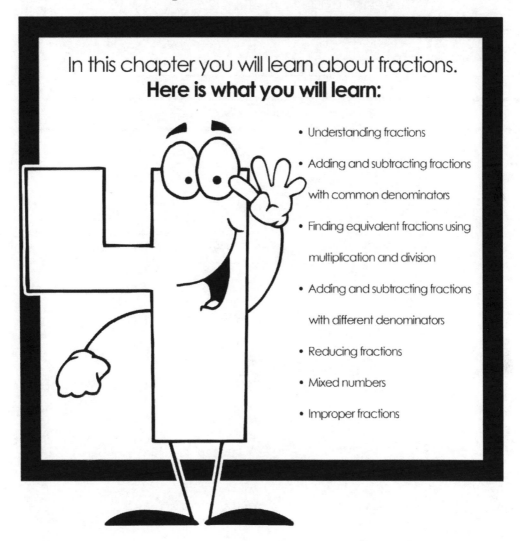

In this chapter you will learn about fractions.
Here is what you will learn:

- Understanding fractions
- Adding and subtracting fractions with common denominators
- Finding equivalent fractions using multiplication and division
- Adding and subtracting fractions with different denominators
- Reducing fractions
- Mixed numbers
- Improper fractions

Lesson 1

Adding Fractions with Common Denominators

To add fractions with common denominators, just add the numerators. The denominators will remain the same.

$$\text{Numerators} \longrightarrow \quad \frac{2}{9} + \frac{3}{9} = \frac{2+3}{9} = \frac{5}{9}$$
$$\text{Common Denominators} \longrightarrow$$

Add the fractions below.

1. $\dfrac{6}{15} + \dfrac{5}{15} + \dfrac{2}{15} = \dfrac{13}{15}$

2. $\dfrac{12}{37} + \dfrac{7}{37} + \dfrac{4}{37} = \underline{\quad}$

3. $\dfrac{13}{80} + \dfrac{9}{80} + \dfrac{27}{80} = \underline{\quad}$

4. $\dfrac{8}{109} + \dfrac{77}{109} + \dfrac{15}{109} = \underline{\quad}$

5. $\dfrac{17}{64} + \dfrac{3}{64} + \dfrac{10}{64} = \underline{\quad}$

6. $\dfrac{3}{21} + \dfrac{7}{21} + \dfrac{4}{21} = \underline{\quad}$

7. $\dfrac{205}{865} + \dfrac{111}{865} + \dfrac{67}{865} = \underline{\quad}$

8. $\dfrac{14}{55} + \dfrac{8}{55} + \dfrac{11}{55} = \underline{\quad}$

9. $\dfrac{2}{13} + \dfrac{7}{13} + \dfrac{1}{13} = \underline{\quad}$

10. $\dfrac{2}{74} + \dfrac{12}{74} + \dfrac{31}{74} = \underline{\quad}$

11. $\dfrac{9}{250} + \dfrac{140}{250} + \dfrac{89}{250} = \underline{\quad}$

12. $\dfrac{3}{94} + \dfrac{3}{94} + \dfrac{1}{94} = \underline{\quad}$

Lesson 2

Subtracting Fractions with Common Denominators

To subtract fractions with common denominators, just subtract the numerators. The denominators will remain the same.

$$\text{Numerators} \longrightarrow \frac{10}{12} - \frac{8}{12} = \frac{10 - 8}{12} = \frac{2}{12}$$
$$\text{Common Denominators} \longrightarrow$$

Subtract the fractions below.

1. $\dfrac{32}{73} - \dfrac{11}{73} = \dfrac{21}{73}$

2. $\dfrac{12}{28} - \dfrac{5}{28} =$ _____

3. $\dfrac{78}{89} - \dfrac{56}{89} =$ _____

4. $\dfrac{112}{146} - \dfrac{92}{146} =$ _____

5. $\dfrac{233}{634} - \dfrac{119}{634} =$ _____

6. $\dfrac{8}{12} - \dfrac{4}{12} =$ _____

7. $\dfrac{608}{759} - \dfrac{325}{759} =$ _____

8. $\dfrac{45}{56} - \dfrac{19}{56} =$ _____

9. $\dfrac{178}{207} - \dfrac{99}{207} =$ _____

10. $\dfrac{30}{49} - \dfrac{17}{49} =$ _____

11. $\dfrac{246}{277} - \dfrac{79}{277} =$ _____

12. $\dfrac{439}{534} - \dfrac{201}{534} =$ _____

13. $\dfrac{77}{88} - \dfrac{11}{88} =$ _____

14. $\dfrac{68}{129} - \dfrac{29}{129} =$ _____

15. $\dfrac{894}{952} - \dfrac{705}{952} =$ _____

Lesson 3

Fraction Word Problems

Write the correct fractions for each question below.

---

1. Daryl is working on his garden. He has planted 28 plants so far. He has 13 tomato plants, 6 eggplants and 9 potato plants. Write the fraction that represents each type of plant.

Tomatoes: $\dfrac{13}{28}$ Eggplants: $\dfrac{6}{28}$ Potatoes: $\dfrac{9}{28}$

2. Mom's favorite hobby is bird watching. Today she saw 15 different birds. She saw 3 blue jays, 9 sparrows, 6 ducks and 1 eagle. Write the fraction that represents each set of birds.

Blue Jays: _____ Sparrows: _____ Ducks: _____ Eagles: _____

3. Johnny went fishing today and caught 17 fish. He caught 2 bass, 6 trout, 5 guppies and 4 goldfish. Write the fraction that represents each type of fish.

Bass: _____ Trout: _____ Guppies: _____ Goldfish: _____

4. Dad is barbequing for the party this afternoon. He has 76 items to cook. He is going to cook 15 hamburgers, 22 chicken wings and 39 sausages.

Hamburgers: _____ Chicken Wings: _____ Sausages: _____

- 70 -

Lesson 4

Equivalent Fractions

 Equivalent Fractions are fractions that have the same value. Even though each shape is divided into a different amount of parts, the shaded parts are equal.

 $\frac{2}{4}$ of the circle is shaded in.

 $\frac{4}{8}$ of the circle is shaded in.

$\frac{2}{4}$ and $\frac{4}{8}$ are equivalent fractions. $\frac{2}{4} = \frac{4}{8}$

Shade in the equivalent fractions on the right to equal the fractions on the left.

 $\frac{1}{4}$ = $\frac{2}{8}$

 $\frac{2}{4}$ = $\frac{4}{8}$

 $\frac{3}{8}$ = $\frac{6}{16}$

 $\frac{5}{8}$ = $\frac{10}{16}$

Lesson 5

Reducing to Equivalent Fractions

- Reducing (or simplifying) fractions means reducing a fraction to an equivalent fraction that has the smallest possible numbers.
- To do this, find the largest number that both the numerator and denominator are divisible by. Then divide both by that number.

Example 1:	Example 2:
$\dfrac{15}{21} \div \left\lfloor\dfrac{3}{3}\right\rfloor = \dfrac{5}{7}$	$\dfrac{12}{20} \div \left\lfloor\dfrac{4}{4}\right\rfloor = \dfrac{3}{5}$
$\dfrac{15}{21} = \dfrac{5}{7}$	$\dfrac{12}{20} = \dfrac{3}{5}$

Reduce the fractions to lowest terms.

1. $\dfrac{18}{27} \div \dfrac{9}{9} = \dfrac{2}{3}$

2. $\dfrac{4}{12} \div \underline{\quad} = \underline{\quad}$

3. $\dfrac{20}{35} \div \underline{\quad} = \underline{\quad}$

4. $\dfrac{9}{24} \div \underline{\quad} = \underline{\quad}$

5. $\dfrac{15}{21} \div \underline{\quad} = \underline{\quad}$

6. $\dfrac{16}{40} \div \underline{\quad} = \underline{\quad}$

7. $\dfrac{10}{25} \div \underline{\quad} = \underline{\quad}$

8. $\dfrac{16}{36} \div \underline{\quad} = \underline{\quad}$

9. $\dfrac{12}{30} \div \underline{\quad} = \underline{\quad}$

10. $\dfrac{9}{27} \div \underline{\quad} = \underline{\quad}$

11. $\dfrac{8}{14} \div \underline{\quad} = \underline{\quad}$

12. $\dfrac{16}{32} \div \underline{\quad} = \underline{\quad}$

- 72 -

Lesson 6

Reducing to Equivalent Fractions with Common Denominators

Before we can add or subtract fractions, we must make sure they have common denominators.
There are two ways to do this--using multiplication or division. Let's look at division first.

$$\frac{9}{12} - \frac{1}{4}$$

In order to subtract these fractions, we must change one to an equivalent fraction with a common denominator (in this case, 4).
To change a fraction to an equivalent fraction, divide the numerator and the denominator by the same number (in this case, 3).

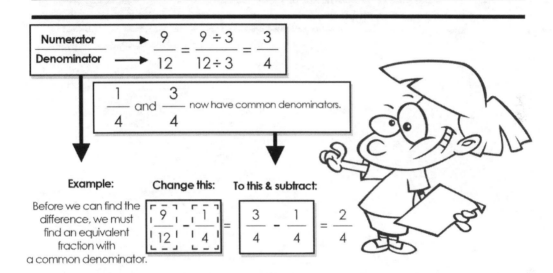

Numerator ⟶
Denominator ⟶
$$\frac{9}{12} = \frac{9 \div 3}{12 \div 3} = \frac{3}{4}$$

$\frac{1}{4}$ and $\frac{3}{4}$ now have common denominators.

Example:

Before we can find the difference, we must find an equivalent fraction with a common denominator.

Change this: **To this & subtract:**

$$\frac{9}{12} - \frac{1}{4} = \frac{3}{4} - \frac{1}{4} = \frac{2}{4}$$

---

1. $\dfrac{6}{10} + \dfrac{1}{5} = \dfrac{3}{5} + \dfrac{1}{5} = \dfrac{4}{5}$

2. $\dfrac{8}{12} + \dfrac{1}{6} = \dfrac{\ \ }{\ \ } + \dfrac{1}{6} = \dfrac{\ \ }{\ \ }$

3. $\dfrac{9}{21} + \dfrac{2}{7} = \dfrac{\ \ }{\ \ } + \dfrac{2}{7} = \dfrac{\ \ }{\ \ }$

4. $\dfrac{12}{32} + \dfrac{3}{8} = \dfrac{\ \ }{\ \ } + \dfrac{3}{8} = \dfrac{\ \ }{\ \ }$

5. $\dfrac{15}{25} - \dfrac{1}{5} = \dfrac{\ \ }{\ \ } - \dfrac{1}{5} = \dfrac{\ \ }{\ \ }$

6. $\dfrac{15}{20} - \dfrac{1}{4} = \dfrac{\ \ }{\ \ } - \dfrac{1}{4} = \dfrac{\ \ }{\ \ }$

7. $\dfrac{25}{35} - \dfrac{3}{7} = \dfrac{\ \ }{\ \ } - \dfrac{3}{7} = \dfrac{\ \ }{\ \ }$

8. $\dfrac{32}{36} - \dfrac{4}{9} = \dfrac{\ \ }{\ \ } - \dfrac{4}{9} = \dfrac{\ \ }{\ \ }$

Lesson 7

Adding Fractions with Different Denominators - Using Division

To add fractions with different denominators, first find a common denominator. Then add the numerators.

Solve each problem. Find each common denominator and sum.

1. $\dfrac{15}{21} = \dfrac{5}{7}$

$+\dfrac{2}{7} = +\dfrac{2}{7}$

$\dfrac{7}{7}$

2. $\dfrac{1}{5} = \underline{}$

$+\dfrac{8}{20} = +\underline{}$

$\underline{}$

3. $\dfrac{21}{30} = \underline{}$

$+\dfrac{2}{10} = +\underline{}$

$\underline{}$

4. $\dfrac{10}{12} = \underline{}$

$+\dfrac{6}{36} = +\underline{}$

$\underline{}$

5. $\dfrac{2}{9} = \underline{}$

$+\dfrac{18}{54} = +\underline{}$

$\underline{}$

6. $\dfrac{25}{35} = \underline{}$

$+\dfrac{2}{7} = +\underline{}$

$\underline{}$

7. $\dfrac{54}{81} = \underline{}$

$+\dfrac{1}{9} = +\underline{}$

$\underline{}$

8. $\dfrac{27}{36} = \underline{}$

$+\dfrac{2}{12} = +\underline{}$

$\underline{}$

9. $\dfrac{6}{7} = \underline{}$

$+\dfrac{28}{49} = +\underline{}$

$\underline{}$

10. $\dfrac{56}{64} = \underline{}$

$+\dfrac{1}{8} = +\underline{}$

$\underline{}$

11. $\dfrac{3}{9} = \underline{}$

$+\dfrac{20}{36} = +\underline{}$

$\underline{}$

12. $\dfrac{81}{90} = \underline{}$

$+\dfrac{7}{10} = +\underline{}$

$\underline{}$

Lesson 8

Subtracting Fractions with Different Denominators - Using Division

To add fractions with different denominators, first find a common denominator. Then add the numerators.

Solve each problem. Find each common denominator and sum.

1.

$$\frac{12}{18} = \frac{12}{18}$$
$$-\frac{2}{9} = \frac{4}{18}$$
$$\frac{8}{18}$$

2.

$$\frac{4}{7} = \frac{}{}$$
$$-\frac{3}{21} = \frac{}{}$$

3.

$$\frac{7}{9} = \frac{}{}$$
$$-\frac{20}{45} = \frac{}{}$$

4.

$$\frac{28}{35} = \frac{}{}$$
$$-\frac{3}{5} = \frac{}{}$$

5.

$$\frac{3}{7} = \frac{}{}$$
$$-\frac{18}{63} = \frac{}{}$$

6.

$$\frac{36}{42} = \frac{}{}$$
$$-\frac{5}{7} = \frac{}{}$$

7.

$$\frac{81}{81} = \frac{}{}$$
$$-\frac{6}{9} = \frac{}{}$$

8.

$$\frac{8}{9} = \frac{}{}$$
$$-\frac{12}{36} = \frac{}{}$$

9.

$$\frac{6}{7} = \frac{}{}$$
$$-\frac{21}{49} = \frac{}{}$$

10.

$$\frac{8}{9} = \frac{}{}$$
$$-\frac{12}{54} = \frac{}{}$$

11.

$$\frac{5}{6} = \frac{}{}$$
$$-\frac{16}{48} = \frac{}{}$$

12.

$$\frac{32}{36} = \frac{}{}$$
$$-\frac{5}{9} = \frac{}{}$$

Lesson 9

Finding Common Denominators using Multiplication 1

Before we can add or subtract fractions, we must make sure they have common denominators. There are two ways to do this--using multiplication or division. Let's look at multiplication .

To change a fraction to an equivalent fraction, multiply the numerator and the denominator by the same number.

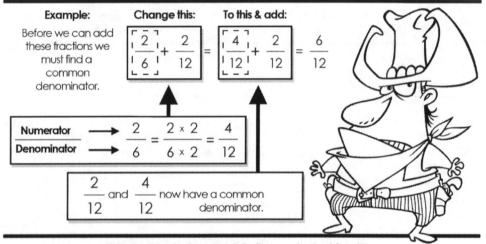

Example:	Change this:	To this & add:
Before we can add these fractions we must find a common denominator.	$\dfrac{2}{6} + \dfrac{2}{12}$ =	$\dfrac{4}{12} + \dfrac{2}{12}$ = $\dfrac{6}{12}$

Numerator ⟶
Denominator ⟶
$$\frac{2}{6} = \frac{2 \times 2}{6 \times 2} = \frac{4}{12}$$

$\dfrac{2}{12}$ and $\dfrac{4}{12}$ now have a common denominator.

Fill in the blanks to complete the equivalent fractions.

1. $\dfrac{2}{6} \times \dfrac{2}{2} = \dfrac{4}{12}$

2. $\dfrac{3}{5} \times \dfrac{\quad}{\quad} = \dfrac{9}{15}$

3. $\dfrac{6}{8} \times \dfrac{\quad}{\quad} = \dfrac{24}{32}$

4. $\dfrac{5}{7} \times \dfrac{\quad}{\quad} = \dfrac{15}{21}$

5. $\dfrac{2}{3} \times \dfrac{\quad}{\quad} = \dfrac{16}{24}$

6. $\dfrac{3}{4} \times \dfrac{\quad}{\quad} = \dfrac{15}{20}$

7. $\dfrac{3}{7} \times \dfrac{\quad}{\quad} = \dfrac{9}{21}$

8. $\dfrac{2}{6} \times \dfrac{\quad}{\quad} = \dfrac{22}{66}$

9. $\dfrac{2}{6} \times \dfrac{\quad}{\quad} = \dfrac{18}{54}$

Lesson 10

Finding Common Denominators Using Multiplication 2

- We just learned that one way to find **equivalent fractions** is to multiply both the numerator and denominator by the same number.

$$\frac{2}{6} = \frac{2 \times 2}{6 \times 2} = \frac{4}{12} \quad \longleftarrow \text{Numerator} \\ \longleftarrow \text{Denominator}$$

- So this means $\dfrac{2}{6} = \dfrac{4}{12}$

$\dfrac{2}{6}$ and $\dfrac{4}{12}$ are now **equivalent fractions**.

Fill in the blanks to make the fractions below equivalent fractions.

1. $\dfrac{3}{5} = \dfrac{}{20}$	2. $\dfrac{2}{4} = \dfrac{6}{}$	3. $\dfrac{1}{2} = \dfrac{}{20}$	4. $\dfrac{6}{8} = \dfrac{30}{}$
5. $\dfrac{1}{7} = \dfrac{}{35}$	6. $\dfrac{2}{6} = \dfrac{30}{}$	7. $\dfrac{4}{5} = \dfrac{}{100}$	8. $\dfrac{2}{4} = \dfrac{}{32}$
9. $\dfrac{4}{12} = \dfrac{}{84}$	10. $\dfrac{5}{10} = \dfrac{45}{}$	11. $\dfrac{3}{7} = \dfrac{6}{}$	12. $\dfrac{3}{5} = \dfrac{33}{}$
13. $\dfrac{9}{16} = \dfrac{72}{}$	14. $\dfrac{1}{3} = \dfrac{}{45}$	15. $\dfrac{15}{25} = \dfrac{30}{}$	16. $\dfrac{16}{18} = \dfrac{}{90}$
17. $\dfrac{3}{16} = \dfrac{}{64}$	18. $\dfrac{3}{5} = \dfrac{}{25}$	19. $\dfrac{4}{6} = \dfrac{4}{}$	20. $\dfrac{2}{8} = \dfrac{4}{}$

Lesson 11

Adding Fractions with Different Denominators - Using Multiplication

To change a fraction to an equivalent fraction, multiply the
numerator and the denominator
by the same number.

Fill in the blanks to find equivalent fractions, then add the fractions.

1. $\dfrac{2}{4} = \dfrac{4}{8}$

$+\dfrac{1}{8} = +\dfrac{1}{8}$

$\qquad \dfrac{5}{8}$

2. $\dfrac{4}{12} = \dfrac{}{12}$

$+\dfrac{3}{6} = +\dfrac{}{12}$

$\qquad \underline{\qquad}$

3. $\dfrac{2}{7} = \dfrac{}{21}$

$+\dfrac{5}{21} = +\dfrac{}{21}$

$\qquad \underline{\qquad}$

4. $\dfrac{4}{28} = \dfrac{}{28}$

$+\dfrac{3}{4} = +\dfrac{}{28}$

$\qquad \underline{\qquad}$

5. $\dfrac{3}{5} = \dfrac{}{50}$

$+\dfrac{12}{50} = +\dfrac{}{50}$

$\qquad \underline{\qquad}$

6. $\dfrac{6}{24} = \dfrac{}{24}$

$+\dfrac{5}{8} = +\dfrac{}{24}$

$\qquad \underline{\qquad}$

7. $\dfrac{21}{48} = \dfrac{}{48}$

$+\dfrac{2}{6} = +\dfrac{}{48}$

$\qquad \underline{\qquad}$

8. $\dfrac{5}{9} = \dfrac{}{81}$

$+\dfrac{12}{81} = +\dfrac{}{81}$

$\qquad \underline{\qquad}$

9. $\dfrac{9}{36} = \dfrac{}{36}$

$+\dfrac{3}{6} = +\dfrac{}{36}$

$\qquad \underline{\qquad}$

10. $\dfrac{4}{9} = \dfrac{}{63}$

$+\dfrac{5}{63} = +\dfrac{}{63}$

$\qquad \underline{\qquad}$

11. $\dfrac{39}{72} = \dfrac{}{72}$

$+\dfrac{3}{9} = +\dfrac{}{72}$

$\qquad \underline{\qquad}$

12. $\dfrac{17}{56} = \dfrac{}{56}$

$+\dfrac{5}{8} = +\dfrac{}{56}$

$\qquad \underline{\qquad}$

Lesson 12

Subtracting Fractions with Different Denominators - Using Multiplication

To change a fraction to an equivalent fraction, multiply the numerator and the denominator by the same number.

Fill in the blanks to find equivalent fractions, then subtract.

1. $\dfrac{2}{4} = \dfrac{10}{20}$

    $-\dfrac{6}{20} = -\dfrac{6}{20}$

    $\dfrac{4}{20}$

2. $\dfrac{14}{15} = \dfrac{}{15}$

    $-\dfrac{4}{5} = -\dfrac{}{15}$

    $\rule{1cm}{0.4pt}$

3. $\dfrac{13}{18} = \dfrac{}{18}$

    $-\dfrac{2}{6} = -\dfrac{}{18}$

    $\rule{1cm}{0.4pt}$

4. $\dfrac{35}{40} = \dfrac{}{40}$

    $-\dfrac{2}{4} = -\dfrac{}{40}$

    $\rule{1cm}{0.4pt}$

5. $\dfrac{5}{6} = \dfrac{}{48}$

    $-\dfrac{29}{48} = -\dfrac{}{48}$

    $\rule{1cm}{0.4pt}$

6. $\dfrac{16}{24} = \dfrac{}{24}$

    $-\dfrac{5}{8} = -\dfrac{}{24}$

    $\rule{1cm}{0.4pt}$

7. $\dfrac{36}{49} = \dfrac{}{49}$

    $-\dfrac{3}{7} = -\dfrac{}{49}$

    $\rule{1cm}{0.4pt}$

8. $\dfrac{5}{6} = \dfrac{}{54}$

    $-\dfrac{29}{54} = -\dfrac{}{54}$

    $\rule{1cm}{0.4pt}$

9. $\dfrac{63}{81} = \dfrac{}{81}$

    $+\dfrac{6}{9} = -\dfrac{}{81}$

    $\rule{1cm}{0.4pt}$

10. $\dfrac{54}{63} = \dfrac{}{63}$

    $-\dfrac{5}{9} = -\dfrac{}{63}$

    $\rule{1cm}{0.4pt}$

11. $\dfrac{27}{48} = \dfrac{}{48}$

    $-\dfrac{4}{8} = -\dfrac{}{48}$

    $\rule{1cm}{0.4pt}$

12. $\dfrac{35}{50} = \dfrac{}{100}$

    $-\dfrac{50}{100} = -\dfrac{}{100}$

    $\rule{1cm}{0.4pt}$

Lesson 13

Mixed Numbers with Common Denominators

When we add or subtract mixed numbers with common denominators, we need to first add or subtract the fractions. Next add or subtract the whole numbers.

Example 1: $2\frac{2}{8} + 6\frac{3}{8}$

Step 1: Add the fractions	**Step 2:** Add the whole numbers
$2\frac{2}{8}$ $\longrightarrow$ $+6\frac{3}{8}$ $\overline{\quad\frac{5}{8}}$	$2\frac{2}{8}$ $\longrightarrow$ $+6\frac{3}{8}$ $\overline{8\frac{5}{8}}$

Example 2: $5\frac{9}{12} - 3\frac{5}{12}$

Step 1: Subtract the fractions	**Step 2:** Subtract the whole numbers
$5\frac{9}{12}$ $\longrightarrow$ $-3\frac{5}{12}$ $\overline{\quad\frac{4}{12}}$	$5\frac{9}{12}$ $\longrightarrow$ $-3\frac{5}{12}$ $\overline{2\frac{4}{12}}$

Add or subtract the mixed numbers below.

---

1. $3\frac{6}{12}$
    $+\,2\frac{4}{12}$
    $\overline{\;5\frac{10}{12}\;}$

2. $5\frac{3}{9}$
    $+\,1\frac{1}{9}$

3. $4\frac{2}{5}$
    $+\,3\frac{2}{5}$

4. $1\frac{8}{23}$
    $+\,1\frac{12}{23}$

5. $9\frac{2}{8}$
    $+\,4\frac{4}{8}$

6. $6\frac{3}{15}$
    $+\,7\frac{7}{15}$

7. $8\frac{21}{39}$
    $+\,5\frac{9}{39}$

8. $3\frac{4}{10}$
    $+\,9\frac{5}{10}$

9. $6\frac{12}{19}$
    $-\,2\frac{7}{19}$

10. $8\frac{7}{8}$
    $-\,5\frac{2}{8}$

11. $10\frac{14}{16}$
    $-\,7\frac{8}{16}$

12. $14\frac{5}{6}$
    $-\,9\frac{1}{6}$

13. $24\frac{21}{25}$
    $-\,19\frac{17}{25}$

14. $36\frac{9}{10}$
    $-\,25\frac{8}{10}$

15. $46\frac{39}{44}$
    $-\,38\frac{12}{44}$

Lesson 14

Reducing Mixed Numbers with Common Denominators

- When we add or subtract mixed numbers with common denominators, first we need to add or subtract the fractions. Next add or subtract the whole numbers.
- When reducing, remember to divide by the largest number possible.

Add or subtract the mixed numbers below, then reduce to the simplest form.

1. $4\frac{3}{10}$
   $+ 1\frac{2}{10}$
   $\overline{}$
   $5\frac{5}{10} = 5\frac{1}{2}$

2. $4\frac{8}{12}$
   $+ 5\frac{1}{12}$

3. $3\frac{2}{18}$
   $+ 6\frac{4}{18}$

4. $3\frac{1}{8}$
   $+ 5\frac{3}{8}$

5. $7\frac{7}{24}$
   $+ 5\frac{5}{24}$

6. $9\frac{10}{36}$
   $+ 6\frac{8}{36}$

7. $4\frac{5}{56}$
   $+ 7\frac{16}{56}$

8. $8\frac{22}{81}$
   $+ 6\frac{23}{81}$

9. $12\frac{10}{16}$
   $- 9\frac{2}{16}$

10. $17\frac{5}{12}$
    $- 5\frac{1}{12}$

11. $11\frac{21}{28}$
    $- 3\frac{7}{28}$

12. $29\frac{9}{9}$
    $-17\frac{3}{9}$

13. $48\frac{37}{42}$
    $- 9\frac{9}{42}$

14. $72\frac{25}{63}$
    $-54\frac{7}{63}$

15. $50\frac{18}{21}$
    $-25\frac{6}{21}$

16. $36\frac{32}{50}$
    $-25\frac{12}{50}$

Lesson 15

Converting Mixed Numbers

To add, subtract, multiply or divide mixed numbers by other fractions, we need to convert the mixed number to an improper fraction.

Step 1:	Step 2:	Step 3:
Multiply the whole number by the denominator.	Add the numerator to the product.	Keep the denominator the same.
$2\frac{1}{4} = \frac{2 \times 4}{4}$	$2\frac{1}{4} = \frac{2 \times 4 + 1}{4} = \frac{9}{4}$	$2\frac{1}{4} = \frac{9}{4}$

Convert each mixed number to an improper fraction.

---

1. $3\frac{4}{3} = \frac{13}{3}$

2. $8\frac{6}{4} = $ —

3. $2\frac{9}{2} = $ —

4. $6\frac{2}{5} = $ —

5. $9\frac{5}{10} = $ —

6. $4\frac{1}{5} = $ —

7. $3\frac{4}{7} = $ —

8. $1\frac{11}{3} = $ —

9. $5\frac{1}{5} = $ —

10. $8\frac{6}{3} = $ —

11. $4\frac{7}{5} = $ —

12. $2\frac{2}{8} = $ —

13. $9\frac{7}{5} = $ —

14. $7\frac{6}{3} = $ —

15. $6\frac{3}{11} = $ —

16. $3\frac{7}{3} = $ —

17. $1\frac{15}{22} = $ —

18. $2\frac{6}{9} = $ —

19. $8\frac{2}{4} = $ —

20. $9\frac{5}{3} = $ —

Lesson 16

Improper Fractions

Improper fractions are fractions that have a numerator greater than or equal to the denominator. Numerator ⟶ 8 49 10 Denominator ⟶ 8 , 7 , 5	To convert an **improper fraction** into a whole number or mixed number, divide the numerator by the denominator. $\dfrac{8}{8} = 8\overline{)8}^{\,1}$ $\dfrac{49}{7} = 7\overline{)49}^{\,7}$ $\dfrac{10}{5} = 5\overline{)10}^{\,2}$	When converting improper fractions, sometimes you get remainders. This means you will get **mixed numbers**. Write the remainder as a fraction with the divisor as the bottom number. $\dfrac{9}{5} = 5\overline{)9}^{\,2\frac{1}{5}} \; \begin{array}{r} -8 \\ \hline 1 \end{array}$

Convert the fractions below.

Convert these fractions to whole numbers:

1. $\dfrac{35}{5} = 7$

2. $\dfrac{12}{3} =$ _____

3. $\dfrac{24}{8} =$ _____

4. $\dfrac{27}{3} =$ _____

5. $\dfrac{48}{6} =$ _____

6. $\dfrac{93}{3} =$ _____

7. $\dfrac{25}{5} =$ _____

8. $\dfrac{84}{2} =$ _____

Convert these fractions to mixed numbers:

9. $\dfrac{15}{6} = 2\dfrac{3}{6}$

10. $\dfrac{10}{4} =$ _____

11. $\dfrac{7}{2} =$ _____

12. $\dfrac{19}{8} =$ _____

13. $\dfrac{23}{4} =$ _____

14. $\dfrac{26}{3} =$ _____

15. $\dfrac{50}{9} =$ _____

16. $\dfrac{46}{8} =$ _____

Chapter 5 - Decimals

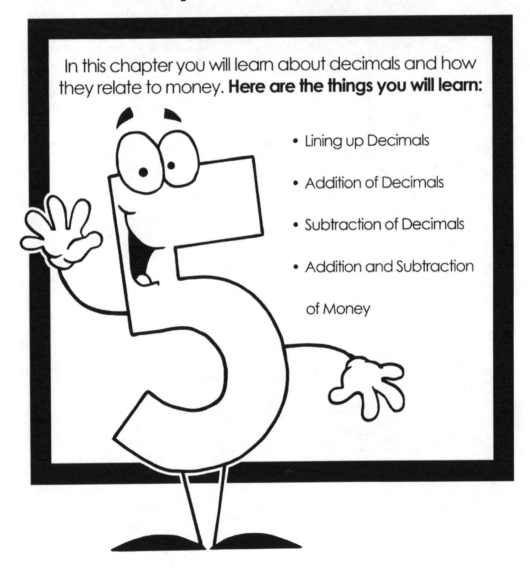

In this chapter you will learn about decimals and how they relate to money. **Here are the things you will learn:**

- Lining up Decimals

- Addition of Decimals

- Subtraction of Decimals

- Addition and Subtraction

of Money

Lesson 1

Decimal Points Addition

Adding decimals is like most normal addition. You just have to remember to line up the decimals.

Hint: Decimal points always go at the end of a whole number (3 = 3.0 or 3.00)

Example: Add 6.33, 5 and 9.5

Step 1: Line up the numbers	**Step 2:** Add zeros	**Step 3:** Find the total
6.33 5. + 9.5	6.33 5.00 + 9.50	6.33 5.00 + 9.50 20.83

Line up the numbers and solve the problems below.
Show your work in the boxes.

1: 5.84 + 1.7 + 3.29

```
   5.84
   1.70
+  3.29
  10.83
```

2: 8.09 + 2.97 + .49

3: 6.94 + 3.07 + 7

4: 24 + 11.09 + 39.74

5: 70.05 + .95 + .38

6: 9.99 + .83 + 60.4

Lesson 2

Arranging and Adding Decimals 1

Use what you learned about adding numbers with decimals to find the totals to the questions below. Show your work in the boxes.

1: 10.54 + 8.01 + .89   **2:** 6.32 + 9.51 + 1.99   **3:** .99 + 5.15 + 12.47

4: 4.21 + 3.57 + 15.05   **5:** 11.97 + 246.1 + 6.50   **6:** .23 + 13.31 + 72.08

7: 61.59 + 31.64 + .08   **8:** 84 + 16.99 + 14.89   **9:** 8.50 + 7.27 + 985

Arranging and Adding Decimals 2

Use what you learned about adding numbers with decimals to find the totals to the questions below. Show your work in the boxes.

1: .154 + 28.46 + 11.751

2: 9.81 + .011 + 6.907

3: 3.645 + 5.707 + 99

4: 6.59 + 1.194 + 5.99

5: 29.175 + 35.19 + 3.809

6: 1.567 + 88.09 + 41.78

7: 58.079 + 44.015 + 7.09

8: 1.955 + 44.19 + 70.091

9: 9.89 + .275 + 67.001

Arranging and Adding Decimals 3

Use what you learned about adding numbers with decimals to find the totals to the questions below. Show your work in the boxes.

1: 164.99 + 805.46 + .75   **2:** 150.92 + 321 + 50.24   **3:** 95.56 + 128.7 + 9.23

4: 389.04 + 84.99 + 6.15   **5:** 18.56 + 991.5 + 525.09   **6:** 61.91 + 571.17 + 223.09

7: 7.56 + 75.61 + 756.1   **8:** 395.1 + 395.11 + 39.51   **9:** 91.8 + 9.18 + 918.8

Lesson 3

Decimal Addition Word Problems

Solve the problems below.

1. Jeremy is a great basketball player. In season one he averaged 9.3 points with 6.2 rebounds per game. In season two he averaged 24.9 points and 3.6 rebounds per game. In season three he averaged 41.2 points with 6.4 rebounds per game. What was the total of his points and rebound averages for all three seasons?

2. Randy eats way too much ice cream. He ate 1.5 ounces on Monday, 2.3 ounces on Tuesday and 3.6 ounces on Wednesday. Thursday he ate 6.9 ounces . Then on Friday he ate 4.2 ounces of ice cream. How much ice cream did Randy eat in total this week?

3. Cynthia has a parrot named Hank. Hank gets his exercise everyday by flying. On Monday he flew 5.1 miles. On Tuesday he flew 6.85 miles. On Wednesday he flew 2.97 miles. Then on Thursday he flew 4.63 miles. How many miles has Hank flown this week?

4. Dad went fishing today. The first fish he caught weighed 12.39 pounds. The second fish he caught weighed 16.05 pounds. The third fish he caught weighed 2.76 pounds. Finally the last fish he caught weighed 9.14 pounds. What is the total weight of all the fish Dad caught today?

Lesson 4

Adding Decimals 1

Find the totals below.

1. 123.47 34.10 + 8.36	**2.** 106.05 23.21 + 1.36	**3.** 253.75 73.36 + 10.15	**4.** 387.12 49.70 + 6.65
5. 513.08 309.12 + 76.59	**6.** 480.21 759.96 + 88.07	**7.** 624.71 267.35 + 20.99	**8.** 945.37 651.83 + 79.41
9. 11.892 20.624 57.393 + 8.102	**10.** .937 13.419 23.757 + 9.144	**11.** 12.587 6.794 90.725 + 24.431	**12.** 67.599 11.180 9.413 + 21.924
13. 22.408 641.119 36.327 + 52.176	**14.** 18.649 97.321 531.655 + 944.299	**15.** 782.113 430.627 67.511 + 12.549	**16.** 72.399 194.912 381.134 + 26.709
17. 11.852 224.379 3.991 + 921.104	**18.** 127.537 363.224 40.916 + 598.644	**19.** 673.112 260.657 167.320 + 6.279	**20.** 587.611 76.435 539.907 + 322.621

Adding Decimals 2

Find the totals below.

1.	651.207	2.	300.498	3.	499.499	4.	549.339
	892.890		53.115		644.466		276.521
	509.001		88.304		320.072		155.277
	37.500		216.224		122.321		608.658
	+ 201.605		+ 366.367		+ 783.009		+ .151

5.	59.650	6.	422.231	7.	500.658	8.	684.942
	324.822		7.807		606.822		29.312
	715.155		725.237		832.615		654.697
	2.777		320.364		299.934		277.347
	+ 500.000		+ 967.957		+ 1.307		+ 306.754

9.	5.001	10.	575.575	11.	229.242	12.	930.854
	470.120		53.347		301.507		292.304
	52.233		699.024		8.111		152.995
	375.032		752.990		358.999		904.654
	+ 960.197		+ 247.367		+ 295.031		+ 35.002

13.	651.133	14.	865.656	15.	966.865	16.	558.715
	326.369		347.211		303.975		669.559
	959.900		122.169		288.361		781.375
	360.452		607.307		465.205		324.278
	+ 995.521		+ 744.654		+ 217.000		+ 587.662

Adding Decimals 3

Find the totals below.

1. 2,418.09
    4,334.49
    712.64
    +1,482.11

2. 6,967.24
    34.13
    5,110.37
    +2,326.22

3. 2,126.94
    3,615.03
    24.77
    +4,331.62

4. 7,269.81
    1,382.43
    409.30
    +   3.99

5. 604.88
    7,291.39
    3,036.13
    +9,123.24

6. 4,168.68
    5,055.33
    4,333.07
    + 659.37

7. 9,224.54
    75.31
    4.52
    +3,012.10

8. 482.00
    3,312.67
    4,999.60
    +   20.54

9. 6,287.90
    961.24
    823.36
    +2,682.48

10. 329.58
    3,677.41
    9,003.36
    +   51.27

11. 7,622.31
    301.02
    440.68
    +2,539.88

12. 5,880.99
    5,951.50
    47.66
    +   9.72

13. 4,408.12
    8,399.99
    254.17
    2,765.55
    +7,321.01

14. 88.78
    9,100.59
    65.34
    3,036.66
    +   7.92

15. 1,448.39
    6,691.15
    2,308.54
    279.02
    +   35.37

16. 5,651.14
    9,842.59
    2,000.77
    2,621.22
    +2,903.00

Lesson 5

Decimal Points Subtraction

Subtracting decimals is like normal subtraction.
You just have to remember to line up the decimals.

Hint: Decimal points always go at the end of a whole number (6 = 6.0 or 6.00)

Example: Subtract 20.99 from 44.5

Step 1: Line up the decimals.	**Step 2:** Add zeros and borrow when needed.	**Step 3:** Subtract all the numbers.
$\begin{array}{r} 44.5 \\ -\ 20.99 \\ \hline \end{array}$	$\begin{array}{r} {}^{3\ 14} \\ 4\cancel{4}.\cancel{5}0 \\ -\ 20.99 \\ \hline \end{array}$	$\begin{array}{r} {}^{3\ 14} \\ 4\cancel{4}.\cancel{5}0 \\ -\ 20.99 \\ \hline 23.51 \end{array}$

Line up the decimals and solve the problems below.
Show your work in the boxes.

1. 9.25 - 4.7

$\begin{array}{r} 9.25 \\ -\ 4.70 \\ \hline 4.55 \end{array}$

2. 30.5 - 17.05

3. 28.12 - .72

4. 605 - 45.07

5. 94.99 - 6.34

6. 339 - 40.09

Lesson 6

Arranging and Subtracting Decimals 1

Subtracting decimals is like normal subtraction. You just have to remember to line up the decimals.

Hint: Decimal points always go at the end of a whole number (6 = 6.0 or 6.00)

Line up the decimals and solve the problems below.

1. 72.53 - 22.56

2. 99.58 - 71.90

3. 33.29 - 19.4

4. 40.06 - 24.1

5. 59.19 - 58.02

6. 82.33 - 51.73

7. 29.23 - 11.06

8. 95.19 - 48.44

9. 80 .46 - 62.9

- 94 -

Arranging and Subtracting Decimals 2

Subtracting decimals is like normal subtraction.
You just have to remember to line up the decimals.

Hint: Decimal points always go at the end of a whole number (6 = 6.0 or 6.00)

Line up the decimals and solve the problems below.

1.   695.53 - 103.08

2.   851.12 - 48.90

3.   305.94 - 12.44

4.   437.2 - 399.56

5.   229.16 - 116.95

6.   821.63 - 354.7

7.   537.21 - 37.59

8.   302.99 - 199.05

9.   900.56 - 621.07

Arranging and Subtracting Decimals 3

Subtracting decimals is like normal subtraction.
You just have to remember to line up the decimals.

Hint: Decimal points always go at the end of a whole number (6 = 6.0 or 6.00)

Line up the decimals and solve the problems below.

1. 81.953 - 2.641

2. 39.058 - 2.806

3. 66.491 - 11.08

4. 68.094 - 7.687

5. 22.916 - 11.695

6. 339.1 - .799

7. 53.210 - 37.059

8. 14 - 7.095

9. 579.802 - .07

Lesson 7

Subtracting Decimals 1

Subtract the amounts below.

1.   231.57
   − 182.24

2.   432.66
   − 106.27

3.   379.20
   − 273.94

4.   628.12
   − 504.39

5.   611.32
   − 369.48

6.   461.30
   − 119.82

7.   654.55
   − 307.47

8.   859.00
   − 689.38

9.   741.99
   − 207.64

10.   584.37
    − 119.01

11.   615.06
    − 527.92

12.   363.19
    − 329.75

13.   64.982
    − 20.191

14.   32.100
    − 12.086

15.   52.604
    − 39.335

16.   11.325
    −   5.425

17.   67.385
    − 46.105

18.   90.488
    − 53.914

19.   75.672
    − 33.127

20.   36.854
    − 11.367

Subtracting Decimals 2

Subtract the amounts below.

1.   1,334.62
   −   451.39

2.   2,485.12
   −   384.67

3.   4,645.14
   −   185.33

4.   3,313.74
   −   599.91

5.   5,482.49
   −   420.24

6.   7,893.72
   −   599.32

7.   6,820.47
   −   875.97

8.   2,339.00
   −   922.11

9.   5,894.27
   −3,554.72

10. 8,775.54
   −3,997.32

11. 7,654.41
   −5,229.80

12. 9,501.64
   −8,329.33

13. 628.399
   −175.508

14. 977.687
   −345.113

15. 710.910
   − 84.456

16. 527.842
   −211.611

17. 139.209
   − 44.364

18. 374.346
   −171.712

19. 452.833
   −299.425

20. 926.001
   −364.967

Subtracting Decimals 3

Subtract the amounts below.

1.   49.9262
   − 32.6139

2.   69.8420
   − 29.9609

3.   39.7124
   − 18.2570

4.   84.4962
   − 38.8691

5.   720.581
   − 556.512

6.   521.003
   − 352.109

7.   120.589
   − 100.075

8.   264.892
   − 155.684

9.   49,078.2
   −38,865.1

10. 8,009.01
   −6,420.57

11. 9,569.25
   −3,365.72

12. 7.65940
   − 2.29995

13. 3,965.21
   −1,788.95

14. 548.722
   − 345.871

15. 2.99265
   − .95846

16. 90.0364
   − 77.8205

17. 89,756.1
   −15,672.7

18. 77,582.1
   −56,963.8

19. 33,587.2
   −19,985.7

20. 9,987.02
   −8,908.25

Lesson 8

Decimal Subtraction Word Problems

Solve the problems below.

1. Mike needs to swim 6 miles a week to get strong enough to make the swim team. On Monday he swam 1.34 miles. On Tuesday he swam 2.49 miles. On Wednesday he swam .82 miles. How much further must he swim to reach his goal of 6 miles?

2. Jenny wants to lift 100 pounds of weight each day. First she lifted 10.57 pounds, then she lifted 29.96 pounds. Next she lifted 32.65 pounds. How much more weight does she need to lift to reach her goal ?

3. Newt needs a total of 300 points on his school projects to go on the field trip. On the first project he scored 86.57 points. On the second project he scored 95.36 points. On the next project he scored 64.11 points. How many more points must he score to go on the trip?

4. James was using so much water playing in the sprinkler that his mom set a limit of 15 gallons per week. On the first day he used 2.65 gallons. On the second day he used 3.21 gallons. On the third day James used 4.81 gallons. Then on the fourth day used 1.92 gallons. How much water does James have left this week?

Lesson 9

Adding Money 1

 The rules that we learned for adding decimals is also how we add money.

$$\begin{array}{r} 289.64 \\ +\ 56.11 \\ \hline 345.75 \end{array} = \begin{array}{r} \$289.64 \\ +\$56.11 \\ \hline \$345.75 \end{array}$$

Find the totals below.

1. $103.32
 + $49.08
 ‾‾‾‾‾‾‾
 $152.40

2. $315.15
 + $12.99

3. $91.64
 + $296.12

4. $144.75
 + $82.32

5. $257.95
 + $189.05

6. $642.44
 + $791.17

7. $309.37
 + $276.24

8. $914.70
 + $367.05

9. $454.12
 $59.99
 + $375.36

10. $708.51
 $623.78
 + $11.63

11. $34.33
 $551.40
 + $186.17

12. $691.11
 $320.95
 + $64.32

13. $111.88
 $965.42
 + $375.30

14. $399.23
 $499.67
 + $233.99

15. $607.14
 $324.24
 + $178.17

16. $119.67
 $394.66
 + $367.92

Adding Money 2

Find the totals below.

1. $108.22
    $399.08
    + $12.28

2. $56.44
    $275.17
    + $2.36

3. $480.55
    $59.63
    + $237.11

4. $365.99
    $264.56
    + $12.00

5. $564.23
    $257.67
    + $106.63

6. $216.21
    $347.96
    + $964.07

7. $754.55
    $191.19
    + $267.67

8. $908.09
    $124.64
    + $573.11

9. $245.77
    $331.06
    $24.33
    + $100.97

10. $210.11
    $772.72
    $186.80
    + $67.29

11. $662.95
    $97.84
    $205.04
    + $177.00

12. $302.34
    $475.62
    $65.24
    + $134.89

13. $905.15
    $465.55
    $992.61
    + $133.21

14. $488.88
    $706.11
    $300.37
    + $511.77

15. $625.33
    $233.31
    $914.45
    + $928.17

16. $723.99
    $949.12
    $811.34
    + $267.09

17. $635.01
    $199.11
    $208.28
    + $322.37

18. $500.49
    $1.11
    $600.59
    + $37.64

19. $368.84
    $675.64
    $99.30
    + $261.71

20. $299.02
    $103.65
    $690.31
    + $782.57

Lesson 10

Subtracting Money 1

Now that you know how to subtract decimals, use what you've learned to answer these money problems.

$$
\begin{array}{r} 15.63 \\ -2.12 \\ \hline 13.51 \end{array}
\quad = \quad
\begin{array}{r} \$15.63 \\ -\$2.12 \\ \hline \$13.51 \end{array}
$$

Subtract the amounts below.

1. $6.22
− $3.84
$2.38

2. $4.70
− $1.35

3. $3.84
− $1.99

4. $7.79
− $5.32

5. $8.84
− $3.53

6. $6.85
− $5.06

7. $9.98
− $6.16

8. $9.27
− $4.64

9. $8.99
− $6.13

10. $3.08
− $.94

11. $7.12
− $5.37

12. $6.39
− $2.17

13. $135.07
− $75.98

14. $209.47
− $105.12

15. $466.17
− $389.55

16. $349.68
− $127.35

17. $859.07
− $407.98

18. $654.00
− $332.37

19. $567.25
− $125.74

20. $804.91
− $722.05

Subtracting Money 2

Subtract the amounts below.

1. $275.29
   − $107.72

2. $535.11
   − $299.39

3. $332.88
   − $111.49

4. $630.00
   − $424.84

5. $643.17
   − $307.51

6. $800.99
   − $115.35

7. $772.63
   − $631.51

8. $704.90
   − $639.17

9. $551.12
   − $337.94

10. $675.99
   − $167.91

11. $240.11
   − $177.54

12. $999.00
   − $327.29

13. $490.17
   − $215.05

14. $807.00
   − $318.37

15. $420.34
   − $385.94

16. $788.40
   − $264.19

17. $711.72
   − $499.07

18. $470.97
   − $295.48

19. $849.84
   − $601.31

20. $511.31
   − $294.52

Lesson 11

Decimal Points Multiplication

To multiply decimals, start by multiplying the numbers just as if they were whole numbers.

Example: Multiply 4.22 by 3.5

Step 1:	Step 2:	Step 3:
Line up the numbers on the right - **do not align the decimal points.**	Starting on the right, multiply each digit in the top number by each digit in the bottom number, just as with whole numbers. Then add the products.	Place the decimal point in the answer by starting at the right and moving the number of places equal to the sum of the decimal places in both numbers multiplied.

Step 1:
```
  4.22
x  3.5
```

Step 2:
```
   4.22
x   3.5
   2110
+12660
  14770
```

Step 3:
```
   4.22  ← 2 decimal places
              +
x   3.5  ← 1 decimal place
   2110
+12660
  14.770  ← 3 decimal places
```

Multiply the problems below and correctly align the decimals.

1.
```
   8.3
 x 6.4
   332
+4980
 53.12
```

2.
```
   3.3
 x 2.9
```

3.
```
   6.7
 x 4.4
```

4.
```
   5.9
 x 3.6
```

5.
```
   4.5
 x 2.9
```

6.
```
   8.5
 x 6.7
```

7.
```
   4.9
 x 2.7
```

8.
```
   9.8
 x 6.2
```

9.
```
   7.7
 x 5.8
```

10.
```
   9.5
 x 8.2
```

11.
```
   8.8
 x 7.4
```

12.
```
   5.9
 x 5.7
```

13.
```
   6.2
 x 4.9
```

14.
```
   4.3
 x 2.5
```

15.
```
   8.7
 x 3.9
```

Lesson 12

Multiplying Decimals 1

Multiply the problems below and correctly align the decimals.

1. 4.2 9
   x 5.3
   2 2.7 3 7

2. 6.8 5
   x .8 6

3. 3.4 2
   x 1.3

4. 5.3 7
   x 6.4

5. 7.3 2
   x 2.6

6. 8 5.5
   x .3 2

7. 6 3.1
   x .5 6

8. 2 9.4
   x 4 9

9. 9.9 9
   x .8 3

10. 6 7.2
    x 2.9

11. .2 4 9
    x .9 7

12. 4 3.3
    x 2 3

13. 5 5.3
    x .5 8

14. 6 8.2
    x 4.3

15. .9 2 7
    x 7.2

16. 7 7.3
    x 2.4

17. 2.4 5
    x .8 4

18. 8 2.7
    x 2.7

19. 5 6.6
    x 9 9

20. 6.0 8
    x .6 7

21. 8.5 2
    x 3.7

22. 5 9.9
    x 6.6

23. 2.8 7
    x 9.4

24. 3 6.2
    x .5 5

25. 9.0 4
    x 4 9

Multiplying Decimals 2

Multiply the problems below and correctly align the decimals.

1. 1 8.3 2
    x   6.8

2. 4 4.0 9
    x   .3 3

3. 2 2.3 9
    x   7 4

4. 5 7.8 2
    x   2.9

5. 7 7.3 2
    x   .5 5

6. 3.4 4 7
    x   4.1

7. 5.7 7 2
    x   5 9

8. 3 3.4 7
    x   3.3

9. 6 6 2.5
    x   1.4

10. 4.2 6 2
    x   5.7

11. 8 2 9 9
    x   .8 8

12. 4 2 9.8
    x   4.1

13. 5.7 2 3
    x   6 3

14. 8 6 4.1
    x   .5 9

15. 9 3.2 2
    x   2.9

16. 7.0 8 5
    x   3 7

17. 3 6 7.5
    x   4.5

18. 9 4.4 7
    x   .8 3

19. 7.2 4 5
    x   7.6

20. 3 2.6 4
    x   5.9

21. 9 9 5.3
    x   8.4

22. 8 1 2 7
    x   .9 9

23. 5.3 3 3
    x   6.6

24. 8 1.2 4
    x   .3 4

25. 9 6.7 7
    x   7.7

Multiplying Decimals 3

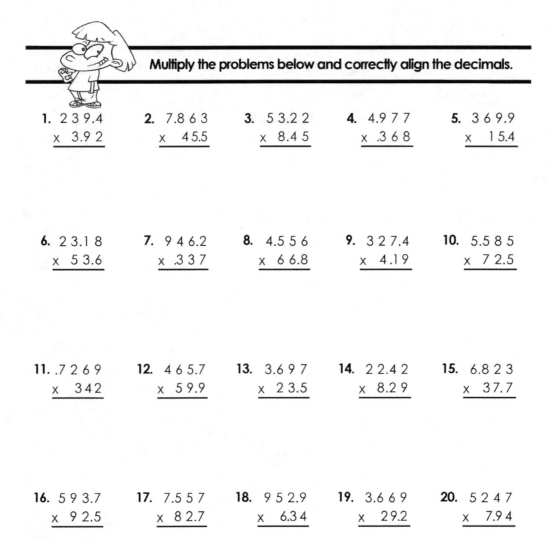

Multiply the problems below and correctly align the decimals.

1. 2 3 9.4
   x 3.9 2

2. 7.8 6 3
   x   4 5.5

3. 5 3.2 2
   x   8.4 5

4. 4.9 7 7
   x .3 6 8

5. 3 6 9.9
   x   1 5.4

6. 2 3.1 8
   x 5 3.6

7. 9 4 6.2
   x .3 3 7

8. 4.5 5 6
   x 6 6.8

9. 3 2 7.4
   x 4.1 9

10. 5.5 8 5
    x 7 2.5

11. .7 2 6 9
    x   3 4 2

12. 4 6 5.7
    x   5 9.9

13. 3.6 9 7
    x 2 3.5

14. 2 2.4 2
    x 8.2 9

15. 6.8 2 3
    x 3 7.7

16. 5 9 3.7
    x 9 2.5

17. 7.5 5 7
    x 8 2.7

18. 9 5 2.9
    x 6.3 4

19. 3.6 6 9
    x 2 9.2

20. 5 2 4 7
    x   7.9 4

Chapter 6 - Geometry

In this chapter you will learn about shapes and geometry. **Here is what you will learn:**

- Identifying Flat Shapes

- Polygons

- Finding Area of Shapes

- Finding Perimeter

- Identifying Solid Shapes

- Understanding Circles

  (Radius, Diameter, Circumference)

- Understanding Points, Lines and Rays

- Understanding Angles

- Understanding Volume

Flat Shapes

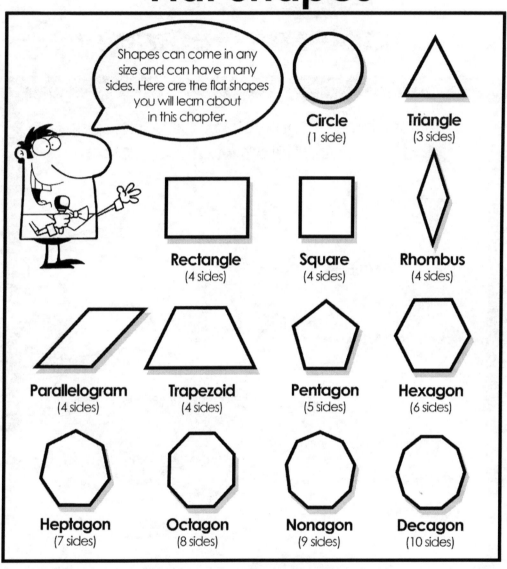

Shapes can come in any size and can have many sides. Here are the flat shapes you will learn about in this chapter.

Circle
(1 side)

Triangle
(3 sides)

Rectangle
(4 sides)

Square
(4 sides)

Rhombus
(4 sides)

Parallelogram
(4 sides)

Trapezoid
(4 sides)

Pentagon
(5 sides)

Hexagon
(6 sides)

Heptagon
(7 sides)

Octagon
(8 sides)

Nonagon
(9 sides)

Decagon
(10 sides)

Lesson 1

Understanding Polygons

- A **polygon** is a closed plane figure made up of 3 or more line segments.
- Polygons that have all sides of equal length are called regular polygons.
- Polygons are named depending on the number of lines that form their boundaries.

Here are some examples of **polygons**:

Triangle:
A polygon with three sides

Quadrilateral
A polygon with four sides.

Pentagon
A polygon with five sides

A **quadrilateral** is a four-sided polygon. Here are some types of **quadrilateral** shapes:

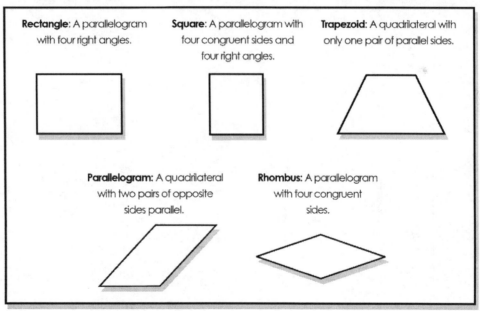

Rectangle: A parallelogram with four right angles.

Square: A parallelogram with four congruent sides and four right angles.

Trapezoid: A quadrilateral with only one pair of parallel sides.

Parallelogram: A quadrilateral with two pairs of opposite sides parallel.

Rhombus: A parallelogram with four congruent sides.

Lesson 2

Finding Area of Squares and Rectangles

Area is the measurement of a shape's surface area.
To find the **area** of a square, multiply the length by the width.

109 ft.

44 ft.

Area = 109 ft. x 44 ft. = 4,796 ft.^{2}
Area = 4,796 ft.^{2}

Find the area of each shape. Write the problem out.

1. 74 in.

74 in.

74in. x 74in. = 5,476 in.^{2}

2. 134 ft.

749 ft.

_____

3.

205 in.   205 in.

_____

4. 299 ft.

436 ft.

_____

5. 637 in.

637 in.

_____

6. 1,262 yd.

507 yd.

_____

Lesson 3

Finding Area of Triangles

To find the **area** of a **triangle** use the formula below:

Area = $\frac{1}{2}$ of base x height

Area = 14in. x 8in. ÷ 2 = 56 in.²

8 in.

14 in.

Find the area of each triangle. Write the problem out.

1.

11 in.

6 in.

2.

12 ft.

17 ft.

3.

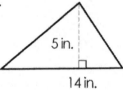

5 in.

14 in.

11in. x 6in. ÷ 2 = 33 in.²

_____

_____

4.

75 in.

46 in.

5.

94 in.

89 in.

6.

112 ft.

156 ft.

_____

_____

_____

Lesson 4

Finding Area of Parallelograms

To find the area of a parallelogram use what we learned before and multiply height times width.

Area = 12 ft. x 9 ft. = 108 ft.^{2}
Area = 108 ft.^{2}

Find the area of each parallelogram. Write the problem out.

1.

6 ft.

6 ft.

2.

13 in.

5 in.

3.

15 ft.

17 ft.

6 ft. x 6 ft. = 36 ft.^{2}
_____   _____

4.

75 ft.

45 ft.

5.

136 in.

115 in.

6.

563 ft.

599 ft.

_____   _____   _____

- 114 -

Lesson 5

Finding Area of Trapezoids

To find the **area** of a **trapezoid** use this formula:

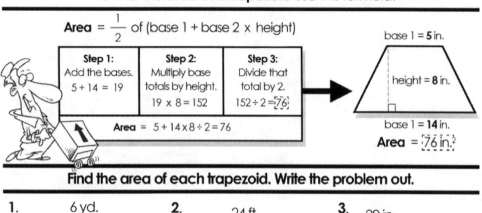

Area = $\frac{1}{2}$ of (base 1 + base 2 x height)

| Step 1: Add the bases. 5 + 14 = 19 | Step 2: Multiply base totals by height. 19 x 8 = 152 | Step 3: Divide that total by 2. 152 ÷ 2 = 76 |

Area = 5 + 14 x 8 ÷ 2 = 76

base 1 = **5** in.
height = **8** in.
base 1 = **14** in.
Area = 76 in.²

Find the area of each trapezoid. Write the problem out.

1.

6 yd.
6 yd.
9 yd.

$6 + 9 \times 6 \div 2 = 45$ yd.²

2.

24 ft.
8 ft.
16 ft.

_____

3.

20 in.
12 in.
32 in.

_____

4.

55 ft.
40 ft.
110 ft.

5.

136 in.
212 in.
175 in.

6.

250 in.
88 in.
210 in.

_____   _____   _____

Lesson 6

Finding Perimeter 1

Perimeter is the distance around an object.
Find the perimeter of each object by adding all the sides.

24 ft.

8 ft.   8 ft.   **Perimeter** = 24 ft. + 20 ft. + 8 ft. + 8 ft. + 2 ft. + 2 ft.

2 ft.   2 ft.   **Perimeter** = 64 ft.

20 ft.

Find the perimeter of each shape. Write the problem out.

1.
55 yd.
36 yd.   42 yd.
67 yd.

2.
125 ft.   89 ft.
125 ft.
89 ft.

3.
123 in.   324 in.
215 in.
107 in.

36 + 67 + 55 + 42 = 197 yd.

_____   _____

4.
75 ft.
101 ft.
347 ft.
289 ft.
62 ft.

5.
572 in.   468 in.
635 in.

6.
917 yd.
234 yd.   705 yd.
917 yd.

_____   _____   _____

Finding Perimeter 2

Find the perimeter of each shape. Write the problem out.

1.
4 yd.
4 yd.
6 yd.
12 yd.
8 yd.
10 yd.

2.
1 ft.
13 ft.
12 ft.
4 ft.
15 ft.

3.
88 in.
96 in.
200 in.
105 in.
88 in.
88 in.
411 in.

4.
8 ft.
8 ft.
8 ft.
8 ft.
8 ft.
8 ft.
8 ft.
8 ft.

5.
20 in.
5 in.
15 in.
20 in.
15 in.
5 in.

6.
4 yd.
17 yd.
35 yd.
20 yd.
19 yd.
15 yd.
4 yd.

7.
55 ft.
60 ft.
34 ft.
27 ft.
10 ft.

8.
7 in.
19 in.
22 in.
18 in.
7 in.
8 in.
23 in.

9.
100 yd.
25 yd.
25 yd.
100 yd.
27 yd.
50 yd.
25 yd.

Lesson 7

Identifying Points, Lines and Rays

A **point** is an exact location in space.	A **line** is an endless straight path.	A **line segment** is a straight path between two points.	A **ray** is a part of a line; it has one endpoint and continues on in one direction.	A **vertex** is a point where two or more rays or line segments meet or cross.

Identify and write how many of each set of figures below.

1.

_____ vertex, 1
_____ ray, 2
_____ point, 2

2.

3.

4.

5.

6.

7.

8.

Lesson 8

Identifying Parts of an Angle

- Angles are determined by points and rays.
- This angle is named - ∠ABC.
- This angle is made up of rays AB and CB.
- The vertex of ∠ABC is the point B.

Identify the vertex, rays and names of each angle.

1.

Angle: _____ABC_____

Vertex: _____B_____

Rays: _____AB, CB_____

2.

Angle: _____

Vertex: _____

Rays: _____

3.

Angle: _____

Vertex: _____

Rays: _____

4.

Angle: _____

Vertex: _____

Rays: _____

5.

Angle: _____

Vertex: _____

Rays: _____

6.

Angle: _____

Vertex: _____

Rays: _____

7.

Angle: _____

Vertex: _____

Rays: _____

8.

Angle: _____

Vertex: _____

Rays: _____

9.

Angle: _____

Vertex: _____

Rays: _____

10.

Angle: _____

Vertex: _____

Rays: _____

11.

Angle: _____

Vertex: _____

Rays: _____

12.

Angle: _____

Vertex: _____

Rays: _____

Solid Shapes

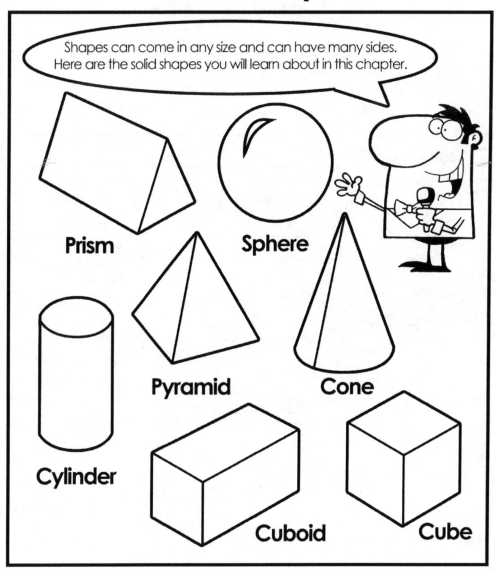

Shapes can come in any size and can have many sides. Here are the solid shapes you will learn about in this chapter.

Prism

Sphere

Pyramid

Cone

Cylinder

Cuboid

Cube

Lesson 9

Identifying Solid Shapes 1

Solid shapes are three-dimensional, non-flat figures. The names of the shapes are determined by the surfaces.

Solid shapes have surfaces, edges and vertices.

Vertex

Edge

Surface

Write the name under each shape and answer the questions below.

1.

  a. How many **vertices** does this shape have? _____

  b. How many **edges** does this shape have? _____

  c. How many **surfaces** does this shape have? _____

  _____

2.

  a. How many **vertices** does this shape have? _____

  b. How many **edges** does this shape have? _____

  c. How many **surfaces** does this shape have? _____

  _____

3.

  a. How many **vertices** does this shape have? _____

  b. How many **edges** does this shape have? _____

  c. How many **surfaces** does this shape have? _____

  _____

Identifying Solid Shapes 2

Solid shapes are three-dimensional, non-flat figures. The names of the shapes are determined by the surfaces.

Solid shapes have surfaces, edges and vertices.

Vertex

Edge

Surface

Write the name under each shape and answer the questions below.

1.

    a. How many **vertices** does this shape have? _____

    b. How many **edges** does this shape have? _____

    c. How many **surfaces** does this shape have? _____

_____

2.

    a. How many **vertices** does this shape have? _____

    b. How many **edges** does this shape have? _____

    c. How many **surfaces** does this shape have? _____

_____

3.

    a. How many **vertices** does this shape have? _____

    b. How many **edges** does this shape have? _____

    c. How many **surfaces** does this shape have? _____

_____

Lesson 10

Circles

Now we will learn about the components that make up a circle. With a circle we have the **radius**, **diameter** and the **circumference**. Knowing these components will help you to solve problems related to circles.

Radius

The **radius** of a circle is the distance from the circle's center point to any point on the circle. It can be used to determine a circle's diameter, circumference and area. Because of the circle's shape, the radius can be drawn in anywhere in the center of the circle.

Use this formula to find the radius of a circle:
Radius = Diameter ÷ 2

Diameter

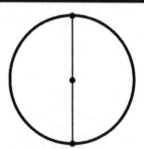

The **diameter** of a circle is the length of a straight line through the center of a circle and touching two points on its edge, the diameter is twice the measurement of the radius. It is the longest distance across the circle. If the diameter of a circle is known, dividing it by two will equal the radius.

Use this formula to find the diameter of a circle:
Diameter = Radius x 2

Circumference

A circle's **circumference** is the distance around the circle. To determine the circumference of a circle, multiply the diameter by pi (π), or multiply the radius by 2 then multiply by pi (π). π is a Greek letter used in math to represent 3.14.

Use this formula to find the diameter of a circle:
Circumference = π x diameter or π x radius x 2

Lesson 11

Identifying Parts of a Circle

Identify the parts of the circles below.

1.

Circle: _____A_____

Radius: ___AB, AC, AD___

Diameter: _____BC_____

2.

Circle: _____

Radius: _____

Diameter: _____

3.

Circle: _____

Radius: _____

Diameter: _____

4.

Circle: _____

Radius: _____

Diameter: _____

5.

Circle: _____

Radius: _____

Diameter: _____

6.

Circle: _____

Radius: _____

Diameter: _____

Lesson 12

Finding the Radius of a Circle

The **radius** of a circle is the distance from the circle's center point to any point on the circle. It can be used to determine a circle's diameter, circumference and area. To find the radius divide the diameter by 2.

Radius = Diameter ÷ 2

Diameter = 12 cm.   Radius = 6 cm.

12 cm.   6 cm.

Radius = 12 ÷ 2 = 6 cm.

Using the diameter, determine the radius of each circle.

1.

18 cm.

Radius: 18 ÷ 2 = 9 cm.

2.

36 in.

Radius: _____

3.

112 ft.

Radius: _____

4.

388 in.

Radius: _____

5.

9.56 ft.

Radius: _____

6.

3.624 cm.

Radius: _____

- 125 -

Lesson 12

Finding the Diameter of a Circle

The **diameter** of a circle is defined as the length of a straight line through the center of a circle and touching two points on its edge, the diameter is twice the measurement of the radius. It is the longest distance across the circle. If the radius of a circle is known, multiplying it by two will equal the diameter.

Diameter = Radius x 2

Radius = 8 cm.   Diameter = 16 cm.

8 cm.   16 cm.

Diameter = 8 x 2 = 16cm.

Using the radius, determine the diameter of each circle.

1.

12 in.

Radius: __12 x 2 = 24 in.__

2.

29 cm.

Radius: _____

3.

89 ft.

Radius: _____

4.

113 cm.

Radius: _____

5.

624 in.

Radius: _____

6.

2,935 ft.

Radius: _____

Lesson 13

Finding the Circumference of a Circle

A circle's **circumference** is the distance around the circle. To determine the circumference of a circle, multiply the diameter by pi (π), or multiply the radius by 2 then multiply by pi (π). π is a Greek letter used in mathematics to represent 3.14.

Radius = 4 cm.   **Diameter** = 8 cm.

4 cm.   8 cm.

Circumference   Circumference
4 x 3.14 x 2 = 25.12   8 x 3.14 = 25.12

Use these formulas to find the circumference of a circle:
Circumference = (π x diameter)   or   (π x radius x 2)
Circumference = (3.14 x diameter)   or   (3.14 x radius x 2)

Using the radius and diameter, determine the circumference of each circle below.

1.
55 in.

Circumference: _____345.4 in._____

2.
72 cm.

Circumference: _____

3.
150 ft.

Circumference: _____

4.
38.5 ft.

Circumference: _____

5.
531.4 in.

Circumference: _____

6.
6.894 cm.

Circumference: _____

Chapter 7 - Graphs

In this chapter you will learn about the different types of graphs.

You will learn to read and create these types of graphs:

- Bar Graphs
- Line Graphs
- Pie Graphs

Graphs

A graph or chart is a diagram used to display data or information visually. There are three types of graphs: **Bar Graphs**, **Line Graphs** and **Pie Graphs**.

In this chapter you will learn to read and create these types of graphs.

A **bar graph** is useful for comparing facts and comparing quantities in different categories.

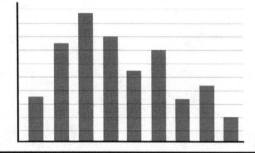

A **line graph** is used to display data or information that changes continuously over time.

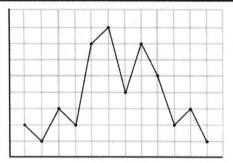

A **pie graph** or **circle graph** shows how the parts of something relate to the whole. It is divided into sectors, where each sector represents a particular category. The sections of this type of graph are usually represented by fractions.

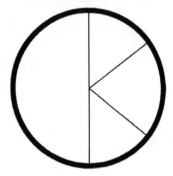

Lesson 1

Reading a Bar Graph 1

Our soccer team did well this year. Here is a graph of the points we scored each game.

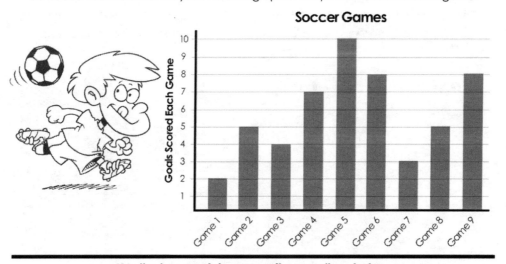

Use the bar graph to answer the questions below.

1. In which game did we score the highest number of goals? _____

2. In which game did we score the lowest number of goals? _____

3. How many goals did we score this entire season? _____

4. In game 9 we scored how many more goals than in game 3? _____

5. In game 5 we scored how many more goals than in game 7? _____

6. In games 2, 3 and 4 we scored how many goals in total? _____

7. In games 4, 5 and 6 we scored how many goals in total? _____

8. In which games did we score the same number of goals? _____

Reading a Bar Graph 2

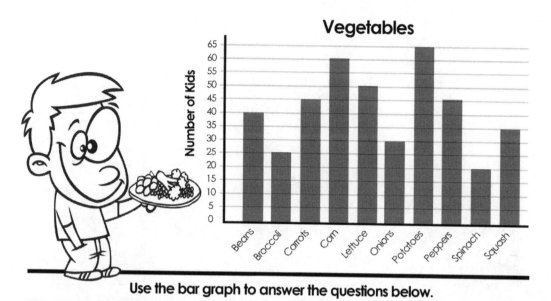

Use the bar graph to answer the questions below.

1. How many kids eat corn? _____

2. How many kids eat squash? _____

3. How many kids eat carrots? _____

4. How many kids eat onions? _____

5. How many kids eat peppers? _____

6. How many kids eat lettuce? _____

7. How many kids eat potatoes? _____

8. How many kids eat broccoli? _____

9. How many kids eat beans? _____

10. How many kids eat spinach? _____

11. How many kids prefer corn over squash? _____

12. How many kids prefer broccoli over spinach? _____

13. How many kids prefer potatoes over beans? _____

14. How many kids prefer lettuce over peppers? _____

15. How many kids prefer carrots over broccoli? _____

16. How many kids prefer corn over onions? _____

17. How many kids prefer potatoes over spinach? _____

18. How many kids prefer beans over onions? _____

Lesson 2

Creating a Bar Graph

Fundraising Totals

Money raised by each student	
Students	**Money**
Mark	$ 50
Jane	$ 15
Steven	$ 60
Suzy	$ 20
Jimmy	$ 35
Mary	$ 65
Thomas	$ 45
Eric	$ 5

Money axis: $ 65, $ 60, $ 55, $ 50, $ 45, $ 40, $ 35, $ 30, $ 25, $ 20, $ 15, $ 10, $ 5, 0

Students axis: Mark Jane Steven Suzy Jimmy Mary Thomas Eric

Use the table above to draw the bar graph, then answer the questions below.

1. How much money did Thomas raise? $_____

2. How much money did Suzy raise? $_____

3. How much money did Jane raise? $_____

4. How much money did Jimmy raise? $_____

5. How much money did Mark raise? $_____

6. How much money did Steven raise? $_____

7. How much money did Mary raise? $_____

8. How much money did Eric raise? $_____

9. Steven raised how much more money than Eric? $_____

10. Suzy needs to raise how much more money to catch up with Jimmy? $_____

11. Mark needs to raise how much more money to catch up with Mary? $_____

12. Steven raised how much more money than Jane ? $_____

13. Suzy needs to raise how much more money to catch up with Mary? $_____

14. Thomas raised how much more money than Jane? $_____

Lesson 3

Comparing Line Graphs

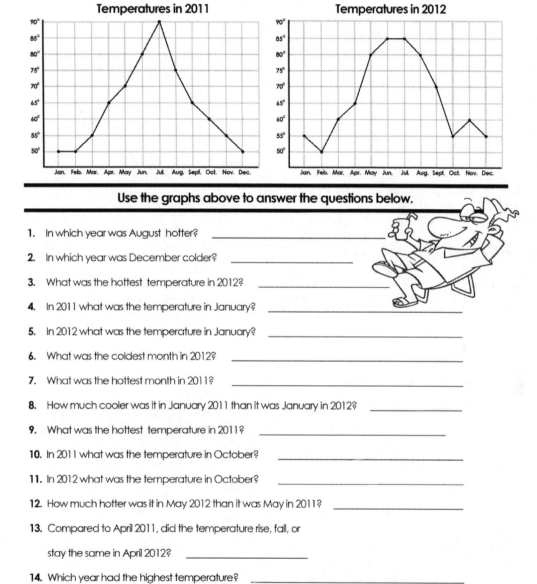

Temperatures in 2011

Temperatures in 2012

Use the graphs above to answer the questions below.

1. In which year was August hotter? _____

2. In which year was December colder? _____

3. What was the hottest temperature in 2012? _____

4. In 2011 what was the temperature in January? _____

5. In 2012 what was the temperature in January? _____

6. What was the coldest month in 2012? _____

7. What was the hottest month in 2011? _____

8. How much cooler was it in January 2011 than it was January in 2012? _____

9. What was the hottest temperature in 2011? _____

10. In 2011 what was the temperature in October? _____

11. In 2012 what was the temperature in October? _____

12. How much hotter was it in May 2012 than it was May in 2011? _____

13. Compared to April 2011, did the temperature rise, fall, or
    stay the same in April 2012? _____

14. Which year had the highest temperature? _____

Lesson 4

Creating a Line Graph

Line graphs use points and lines to show data visually.

Use the data on the left to draw your own line graph.
First plot the points, then draw a line connecting the points

Numbers of People in Museum	
Time	**People**
9 am	20
10 am	55
11 am	30
12 pm	10
1 pm	45
2 pm	65
3 pm	60
4 pm	40
5 pm	55
6 pm	15

Museum Attendance

Use the line graph you just drew to answer the questions below.

1. At what time was the attendance in the museum the highest? _____

2. At what time was the attendance in the museum the lowest? _____

3. How many people were in the museum at noon? _____

4. How many people were in the museum at 9am? _____

5. How many people were in the museum at 4pm? _____

6. How many more people were the in the museum at 5pm compared to 11am? _____

7. From 1pm to 2pm, how many people showed up at the museum? _____

8. From 5pm to 6pm, how many people left the museum? _____

9. During what one-hour time period did the attendance increase the most? _____

10. During what one-hour time period did the attendance decrease the most? _____

Lesson 5

Identifying Points on a Graph

Graphs are used to show information in a visual form.

Using the graph above, write out the points that make up each shape.

1. _A10, C10, C7, E7_____ 2. _____

3. _____ 4. _____

5. _____ 6. _____

7. _____ 8. _____

9. _____ 10. _____

Lesson 6

Plotting Points on a Graph

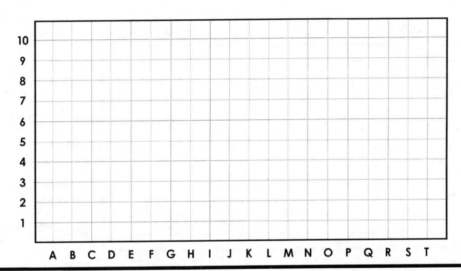

Using the coordinates below, plot the points on the graph above.
Draw a line between the points on the graph to create geometric shapes
and the write the name for each shape in the blanks.

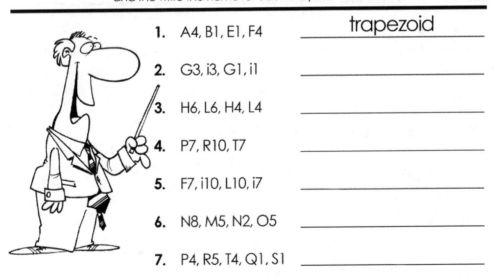

1. A4, B1, E1, F4   trapezoid

2. G3, i3, G1, i1   _____

3. H6, L6, H4, L4   _____

4. P7, R10, T7   _____

5. F7, i10, L10, i7   _____

6. N8, M5, N2, O5   _____

7. P4, R5, T4, Q1, S1   _____

Lesson 7

Reading a Pie Chart 1

A **pie graph** shows how the parts of something relate to the whole.
It is divided into sectors. Each sector represents a particular category.

Use the graphs below to answer the questions.

Students' Favorite Classes

Kids' Favorite Pets

1. Which class do the students like most?

   _____

2. Which class do the students like the least?

   _____

3. What is the second-favorite class?

   _____

4. Which class do the students like more, math or reading?

   _____

5. What is the kids' favorite pet?

   _____

6. What is the kids' least favorite pet?

   _____

7. What is the kids' second favorite pet?

   _____

8. Do more kids' want a gerbil or fish?

   _____

Lesson 8

Reading a Pie Chart 2a

Shoe types that family members prefer.

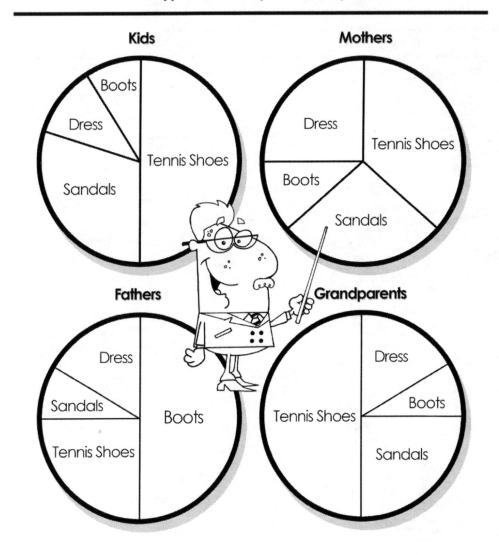

Lesson 9

Reading a Pie Chart 2b

Use the pie charts on the last page to answer the questions below.

1. Which shoes do kids like the most? _____

2. Which shoes do grandparents like the most? _____

3. Which shoes do mothers like the most? _____

4. Which shoes do fathers like the most? _____

5. What is the kids' second favorite shoes? _____

6. What is the fathers' second favorite shoes? _____

7. Which shoes do kids like least? _____

8. Which shoes do grandparents like least? _____

9. Which shoes do mothers like least? _____

10. Which shoes do fathers like least? _____

Lesson 10

Creating a Pie Chart

 A **pie graph** shows how the parts of something relate to the whole. It is divided into sectors. Each sector represents a particular category. The sum of all the parts will always equal 100%.

Using the information below, fill in the pie graphs with the correct numbers.

Most Studied Planets

1. Mars - 50%

2. Mercury - 6%

3. Venus - 10%

4. Neptune - 34%

How Students Get to School

1. School Bus - 42%

2. Car - 35%

3. Bike - 15%

4. Walk - 8%

Favorite Movie Types in Schools

1. Comedy - 35%

2. Action - 18%

3. Drama - 8%

4. Animation - 24%

5. Science Fiction- 15%

Fish Population in the Pond

1. Bass - 20%

2. Catfish - 27%

3. Trout - 14%

4. Guppies - 32%

5. Turtles - 7%

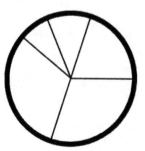

Practice Test #1

Practice Questions

1. What is the value of the digit 5 in the number 3,456,789?

Ⓐ Fifty thousand

Ⓑ Five thousand

Ⓒ Five-hundred thousand

Ⓓ Five million

2. In ice hockey, the number of points a player scores is defined as the sum of the number of goals and the number of assists. Which hockey player listed in the table below has the highest number of points?

Player	Goals	Assists
Phillips	2	23
Jackson	5	17
Robinson	13	15
Miller	8	19

Ⓐ Phillips

Ⓑ Jackson

Ⓒ Robinson

Ⓓ Miller

3. A recipe calls for $3\frac{3}{4}$ cups of flour. Which fraction below is equivalent to this amount?

Ⓐ $\frac{5}{2}$

Ⓑ $\frac{15}{4}$

Ⓒ $\frac{3}{2}$

Ⓓ $\frac{9}{4}$

4. One morning a total of 151 eggs are collected from a henhouse. The eggs are packed in cartons of 12 for shipment. How many eggs are remaining after as many cartons as possible are packed?

Ⓐ 3

Ⓑ 9

Ⓒ 7

Ⓓ 1

5. Which numeral is in the thousandths place in 0.3874?

Ⓐ 3

Ⓑ 8

Ⓒ 7

Ⓓ 4

6. A rectangular plot in a garden is three times longer than it is wide. What is the perimeter of the garden if it has a width of 8 meters?

Ⓐ 32 meters

Ⓑ 192 meters

Ⓒ 24 meters

Ⓓ 64 meters

7. The number of customers in a new restaurant is given in the table below:

Week	Customers
1	155
2	180
3	205

Part A: How many customers should be expected in week 4?

Ⓐ 225

Ⓑ 230

Ⓒ 200

Ⓓ 255

Part B: The average meal at the restaurant is $12. How much money will they make in week 4? Explain your process.

_____

_____

_____

8. The rectangular prism below has a volume of 144 cu. cm. The length and width are given below. What is the height of the rectangular prism?

? cm

6 cm

8 cm

9. 0.58 - 0.39=

Ⓐ 0.19

Ⓑ 1.9

Ⓒ 0.29

Ⓓ 2.9

10. The recipe Mary is using to bake cupcakes requires 1 cup of milk and makes 8 cupcakes. If she needs to make 32 cupcakes for the party, how much milk is needed?

Ⓐ 1 pint

Ⓑ 1 gallon

Ⓒ 3 cups

Ⓓ 1 quart

11. Solve the equation: $\frac{2}{5} + \frac{3}{4} - \frac{1}{2} = ?$

---

12. Which of the following is correct? Explain your answer.

Ⓐ $\frac{4}{7} = \frac{12}{21}$

Ⓑ $\frac{3}{4} = \frac{12}{20}$

Ⓒ $\frac{5}{8} = \frac{15}{32}$

Ⓓ $\frac{7}{9} = \frac{28}{35}$

---

13. Donnie has a baseball card that is 4.2 inches tall and 2.6 inches wide. What is the area of the card?

---

14. An electronics store sells *E* Evercell brand batteries in packages of 4 and *D* Durapower brand batteries in packages of 6. Which expression represents the total number of batteries in the store?

    Ⓐ $(4 + E) \times (6 + D)$

    Ⓑ $(4 \times E) + (6 \times D)$

    Ⓒ $(4 + E) + (6 + D)$

    Ⓓ $(4 \times E) \div (6 \times D)$

15. At the park there is a walking trail that goes around the perimeter. One lap around the park is .28 miles. Samantha walks 11 laps. How far has she walked?

16. Solve the equations below:

$.3 \times 1.25 =?$

$1.22 - .85 + .34 =?$

$(.22 + 1.48) \times .5 =?$

17. Given the figure of the parallelogram below, which side is parallel to side $\overline{RT}$?

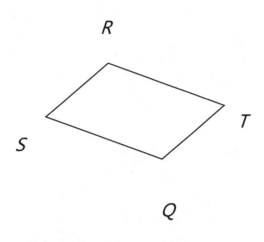

Ⓐ $\overline{RS}$

Ⓑ $\overline{QS}$

Ⓒ $\overline{QT}$

Ⓓ None of the above

18. A fish tank is a rectangular prism with a length of 7 inches and a width of 5 inches and can hold a volume of 210 cubic inches of water. What is the height of the tank?

Ⓐ 6 inches

Ⓑ 5 inches

Ⓒ 17.5 inches

Ⓓ 10 inches

19. The all-time rushing leader in professional football ran for 18,335 yards in his career. What is the best whole number approximation of the number of miles he ran?

20. A survey of a random sample of 100 drivers asked them the color of their car. The results of the survey are presented in the table below.

Color of car	Number of drivers
Blue	26
Red	14
Yellow	36
Silver	24

If the parking lot at the local store is filled with 25 cars, how many yellow cars would be expected to be in the lot?

Ⓐ 6

Ⓑ 9

Ⓒ 11

Ⓓ 12

21. Cindy earned \$100 one week at the ice cream stand. She put $\frac{1}{4}$ of the money in her savings account and kept the rest as cash. After this, she received a cash bonus of \$20 from the owner of the ice cream stand and didn't put any of it in the savings account. Which expression represents the amount of cash Cindy currently has?

Ⓐ $C = \frac{3}{4}(100) + 20$

Ⓑ $C = \frac{1}{4}(100) + 20$

Ⓒ $C = \frac{1}{4}(100) - 20$

Ⓓ $C = \frac{3}{4}(120)$

22. Mr. Thompson fills his 25.2 gallon gasoline tank with gas that costs $2.98 a gallon. Which is the best approximation of the cost of the gasoline?

Ⓐ $50

Ⓑ $60

Ⓒ $75

Ⓓ $90

23. Using the order of operations solve the problem below.

$8 \times (5 - 2) + (4 + 5) =$ _____

24. Janice gets home from school at 2:45 PM. She does homework for 1 hour and 30 minutes, then goes out and plays for 1 hour and 45 minutes before returning home for dinner. What time is it when Janice returns home for dinner?

Ⓐ

Ⓑ

Ⓒ

Ⓓ

25. Two sisters were arguing who could have a larger piece of pie. Their mother told the older daughter she could have 2/5 of the pie. She told the younger daughter she could have 1/3 of the pie. Which daughter received a larger piece of pie?

Ⓐ The older daughter.

Ⓑ The younger daughter

Ⓒ Same size piece for each daughter

Ⓓ Not enough information to determine

26. It takes Jack 14.67 minutes to get to school in the morning. It only takes Clayton 10.24 minutes to get to school. How much less time does it take Jack to get to school?

27. A ship is located on the map at coordinates (4, 9). If the radar indicates the lighthouse is 5 units east and 4 units south of the ship, what is the location of the lighthouse?

North

Ⓐ (9, 5)

Ⓑ (9, 4)

Ⓒ (8, 3)

Ⓓ (9, 13)

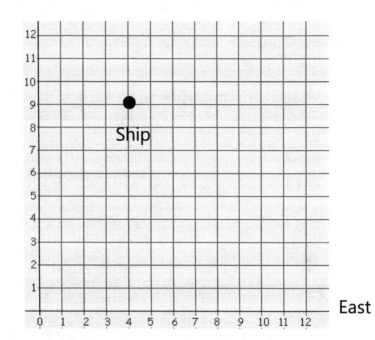

East

28. When taking a person's temperature with an oral thermometer, temperatures between 96.9° and 99.5° are considered normal. Which temperature below is outside of the normal range?

Ⓐ 97.2°

Ⓑ 99.3°

Ⓒ 98.9°

Ⓓ 96.3°

29. The high temperatures in degrees Celsius for a work week are given on the table below:

Day	Monday	Tuesday	Wednesday	Thursday	Friday
High Temp.	9	16	13	20	22

What was the mean high temperature for the week?

Ⓐ 14

Ⓑ 16

Ⓒ 13

Ⓓ 22

30. On the graph below plot the points (6,9), (3,8), and (-2,4).

31. A little league has 92 children sign up for baseball season. If each team needs at least 14 players, how many complete baseball teams can be formed?

Ⓐ 5

Ⓑ 6

Ⓒ 7

Ⓓ 8

32. Part A: Given the isosceles trapezoid PQRS below, which two sides are congruent?

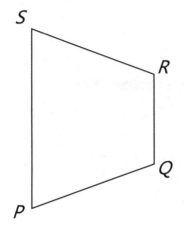

Ⓐ $\overline{PS}$ and $\overline{QR}$

Ⓑ $\overline{RS}$ and $\overline{QP}$

Ⓒ $\overline{QP}$ and $\overline{RQ}$

Ⓓ $\overline{PS}$ and $\overline{RS}$

Part B: Which two sides are parallel?

Ⓐ $\overline{PS}$ and $\overline{QR}$

Ⓑ $\overline{RS}$ and $\overline{QP}$

Ⓒ $\overline{QP}$ and $\overline{RQ}$

Ⓓ $\overline{PS}$ and $\overline{RS}$

33. A length of string is measured to be $\frac{31}{8}$ inches. Between which two points on the ruler below will this length lie?

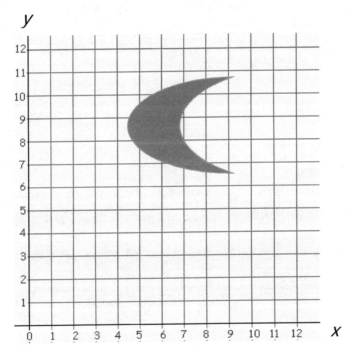

Ⓐ Between points A and B

Ⓑ Between points B and C

Ⓒ Between points C and D

Ⓓ Between points D and E

34. Which point lies within the shaded region below?

Ⓐ (5, 6)

Ⓑ (8, 6)

Ⓒ (7, 10)

Ⓓ (9, 9)

- 154 -

35. The model shown below represents $1\frac{7}{10}$

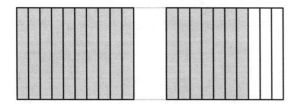

Which decimal does this also represent?

Ⓐ 0.7

Ⓑ 0.07

Ⓒ 1.7

Ⓓ 1.07

36. An electronics store sells T.V.'s for \$525 and game systems for \$250. If 36 people buy T.V. and 29 people buy a game system how much money would the store make?

37. Of the 20 people in Joan's class, 4 of them have birthdays in the winter, 7 have birthdays in the spring, 3 have birthdays in the summer, and 6 have birthdays in the fall. What is the probability a student chosen at random will have a birthday in either the spring or the summer?

Ⓐ $\frac{7}{20}$

Ⓑ $\frac{1}{2}$

Ⓒ $\frac{3}{20}$

Ⓓ $\frac{3}{10}$

38. Phil is going to school overseas for 9 weeks and 5 days. How many days will Phil be gone?

Ⓐ 95

Ⓑ 44

Ⓒ 59

Ⓓ 68

39. Julie shopped for first-aid cream. One large tube held 1.5 fluid ounces and the smallest tube held 0.33 fluid ounces. What is the difference in the number of fluid ounces of cream in the two tubes?

Ⓐ 1.8

Ⓑ 1.27

Ⓒ 1.23

Ⓓ 1.17

40. Jan played a game which used a fair spinner like the one shown here. Jan needs the arrow to land on green on her next turn.

What is the probability that the arrow lands on green when Jan spins one time?

Ⓐ $\frac{1}{6}$

Ⓑ $\frac{1}{3}$

Ⓒ $\frac{1}{2}$

Ⓓ $\frac{2}{3}$

Practice Test #2

Practice Questions

1. Which number represents "fifty-seven thousand three hundred and forty"?

Ⓐ 570,340

Ⓑ 573,400

Ⓒ 5,734

Ⓓ 57,340

2. Four students were given a typing test measuring their speed in words per minute and then given the same typing test several weeks later. Which student had the greatest improvement?

Student	First score (words per minute)	Second score (words per minute)
Alexander	22	39
Betty	39	48
Carolyn	27	43
David	22	42

Ⓐ Alexander

Ⓑ Betty

Ⓒ Carolyn

Ⓓ David

3. A bookshelf is to be $7\frac{5}{8}$ inches wide. Which fraction below is equivalent to this measurement?

Ⓐ $\frac{35}{8}$

Ⓑ $\frac{75}{8}$

Ⓒ $\frac{61}{8}$

Ⓓ $\frac{43}{8}$

4. Toasty Donut Shop makes 141 donuts one morning. The donuts are packaged in boxes of 12 for delivery. How many single donuts are left over?

Ⓐ 3

Ⓑ 9

Ⓒ 6

Ⓓ 1

5. Which numeral is in the thousandths place in .5643?

Ⓐ 5

Ⓑ 6

Ⓒ 4

Ⓓ 3

6. Dennis weighs 56 pounds. His little brother Donny weighs 23 pounds less than him. What is Donny's weight in ounces?

_____

_____

_____

7. A square flower garden has an area of 81 feet. What is the length of one side of the garden?

Ⓐ 9 feet

Ⓑ 20.25 feet

Ⓒ 40.5 feet

Ⓓ 324 feet

8. Which of the following is correct?

Ⓐ $\dfrac{2}{3} = \dfrac{18}{24}$

Ⓑ $\dfrac{4}{5} = \dfrac{16}{20}$

Ⓒ $\dfrac{1}{9} = \dfrac{4}{18}$

Ⓓ $\dfrac{3}{8} = \dfrac{9}{16}$

9. Round each of the decimals below to the nearest hundredth.

3.116 ≈ _____

3.081 ≈ _____

3.006 ≈ _____

3.107 ≈ _____

10. Which of the following figures is a trapezoid?

Ⓐ

Ⓑ

Ⓒ

Ⓓ

11. A gallon of cooking oil is used to make popcorn for 256 people. How much cooking oil is needed to make popcorn for 96 people?

Ⓐ 2 quarts

Ⓑ 3 pints

Ⓒ 1 quart

Ⓓ 1 cup

12. Jodi made a sum of money yesterday at a bake sale. She spent half of the money to buy more ingredients for next week's bake sale, and then spent $12 to go to the movies. Jodi has $17 remaining. How much did she make yesterday at the bake sale?

Ⓐ $36

Ⓑ $58

Ⓒ $46

Ⓓ $41

13. Express 99/14 as a mixed fraction.

Ⓐ $7\frac{1}{14}$

Ⓑ $7\frac{3}{14}$

Ⓒ $7\frac{11}{14}$

Ⓓ $7\frac{5}{14}$

14. A little boy decides to give away all of his marbles. Each of his 4 friends is to receive an equal share. Which of the statements below describes how this can be done?

Ⓐ Multiply his marbles by 4 and give this amount to each of his friends

Ⓑ Multiply his marbles by 2 and give this amount to each of his friends

Ⓒ Multiply his marbles by 1/2 and give this amount to each of his friends

Ⓓ Multiply his marbles by 1/4 and give this amount to each of his friends

15. Part A: A store receives regular shipments of paper towels. Each shipment contains 26 boxes. Each box contains 6 packages and each package has 8 rolls of paper towels. How many rolls of paper towels come in one shipment?

Part B: If the store sells 6100 rolls each month how many shipments will it need in one month?

16. Part A: A zoo has three different lion enclosures. The first one is $\frac{5}{8}$ of an acre. The second one is $\frac{5}{6}$ of an acre. How much bigger is the second on than the first one?

Part B: If the third one is $\frac{7}{12}$, what is the total number of acres in all three enclosures?

17. Given the figure of the parallelogram below, which side is congruent to side $\overline{RT}$?

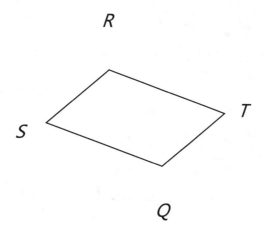

Ⓐ $\overline{RS}$

Ⓑ $\overline{QS}$

Ⓒ $\overline{QT}$

Ⓓ None of the above

18. A large rectangular-prism-shaped tank at the zoo is 8 feet wide and 5 feet high. How long is the tank if it holds a volume of 200 cubic feet of water?

Ⓐ 8 feet

Ⓑ 6 feet

Ⓒ 13 feet

Ⓓ 5 feet

19. Mount McKinley, the tallest mountain in North America, is 20,320 feet high. Approximately how many miles tall is the Mount?

Ⓐ 6

Ⓑ 5

Ⓒ 4

Ⓓ 3

20. Mrs. Jackson records the hair color of the 20 children in her room and obtains the following results:

Hair color	Number of students
Black	6
Brown	8
Blonde	4
Red	2

If the school has a total of 240 children, how many children with brown hair should be expected?

21. A grocery store determines the price of a gallon milk, *P*, in dollars will be determined by multiplying the wholesale price, *W*, in dollars by 1.5 and adding 25 cents. Which expression below represents this relationship?

Ⓐ $P = 1.5 + W + 0.25$

Ⓑ $P = 0.25W + 1.5$

Ⓒ $P = 1.75W$

Ⓓ $P = 1.5W + 0.25$

22. The movie Laura went to see ended at 8:15 PM. The movie she saw was 2 hours and 45 minutes long. What time did the movie start?

Ⓐ

Ⓑ

Ⓒ

Ⓓ

23. Using order of operations solve the problem below.

$$3 + (9 - 4) \times (4 + 5) = ?$$

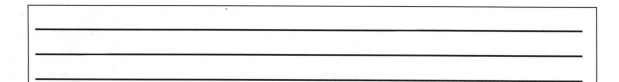

24. On Saturday Allen spent 73 minutes mowing the grass. He spent 42 minutes washing his car, another 56 minutes repairing a fence, and 31 minutes trimming the shrubs. How much time did he spend doing chores on Saturday?

Ⓐ 2 hours 51 minutes

Ⓑ 3 hours 22 minutes

Ⓒ 3 hours 18 minutes

Ⓓ 3 hours 28 minutes

25. Which one of the statements about the rectangular prism below is FALSE?

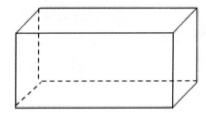

Ⓐ There are 12 edges on the rectangular prism.

Ⓑ The six sides of the rectangular prism all have the same area.

Ⓒ Some of the edges are parallel.

Ⓓ There are 8 vertices on the rectangular prism.

26. The model shown below represents $1\frac{5}{10}$

Which decimal does this also represent?

Ⓐ 0.5

Ⓑ 1.5

Ⓒ 1.05

Ⓓ 1.005

27. An observation tower is located at point (8, 5) on the map grid below. A fire is observed from a location 4 units west and 2 units north of the tower. What is the location of the fire?

Ⓐ (12, 7)

Ⓑ (4, 7)

Ⓒ (6, 9)

Ⓓ (4, 5)

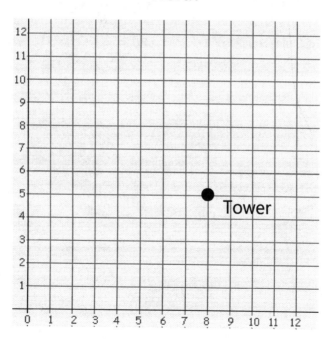

28. Maria is moving and needs a box to pack books in. The box needs to be 416 cubic inches. Which of the following boxes is the right size?

Ⓐ a box that is 8 $in.\times$ 12 $in.\times$ 5 $in.$

Ⓑ a box that is 12 $in.\times$ 4 $in.\times$ 9 $in.$

Ⓒ a box that is 13 $in.\times$ 5 $in.\times$ 7 $in.$

Ⓓ a box that is 13 $in.\times$ 4 $in.\times$ 8 $in.$

29. The number of washes the Squeaky Clean car wash made last week is given in the table below:

Day	Monday	Tuesday	Wednesday	Thursday	Friday
Car Washes	22	28	38	47	45

What is the mean number of car washes for the week?

Ⓐ 44

Ⓑ 47

Ⓒ 36

Ⓓ 31

30. 0.28 x 0.17

Ⓐ 0.2260

Ⓑ 0.4760

Ⓒ 0.0226

Ⓓ 0.0476

31. Jim brings two ice chests to the beach. Ice chest A has two compartments, while Ice Chest B just has one. Ice chest B can hold 24 drinks while Ice chest A can hold twice as many. If the larger compartment in Ice Chest A holds 34, how many does the smaller one hold?

_____
_____
_____

32. Mandy's Farmer's Market sells pears in boxes of 18. A shipment of 417 pears arrives that morning. How many full boxes of pears can Mandy sell using that shipment?

Ⓐ 25

Ⓑ 23

Ⓒ 18

Ⓓ 20

33. The side length of a regular pentagon is 6.5 centimeters. What is the perimeter of this figure?

Ⓐ 26.0 cm.

Ⓑ 42.25 cm.

Ⓒ 39.0 cm.

Ⓓ 32.5 cm.

34. A length of yarn is measured to be $\frac{35}{8}$ inches. Between which points on the ruler will this length lie?

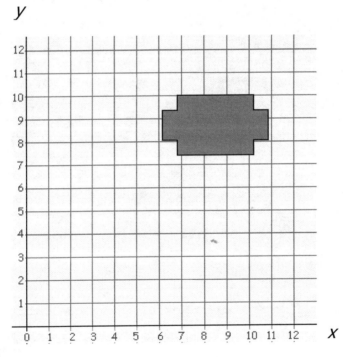

Ⓐ Between points A and B

Ⓑ Between points B and C

Ⓒ Between points C and D

Ⓓ Between points D and E

35. Which point lies within the shaded region below?

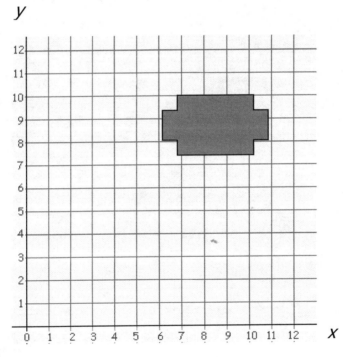

Ⓐ (5, 8)

Ⓑ (8, 9)

Ⓒ (7, 11)

Ⓓ (9, 7)

36. The workers at a large construction site were made up of 11 plumbers, 7 electricians, 13 carpenters, 8 concrete finishers and 11 laborers. What is the probability that a worker chosen at random will be either a carpenter or an electrician?

Ⓐ $\frac{13}{50}$

Ⓑ $\frac{9}{25}$

Ⓒ $\frac{2}{5}$

Ⓓ $\frac{7}{25}$

37. Which line graph correctly reflects the data shown in the table?

Time	Number of Customers
2:00 pm	20
4:00 pm	30
6:00 pm	50
8:00 pm	10

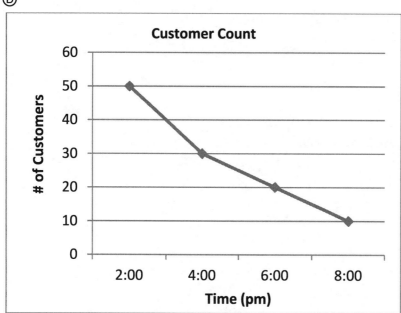

38. Four students measured the length of the pencil each was using. The list shows the lengths, in centimeters, of the four pencils.
17.03 cm, 17.4 cm, 17.31 cm, 17.09 cm

Which list shows the lengths of the pencils in order, from shortest to longest?

Ⓐ *17.4 cm, 17.31 cm, 17.09 cm, 17.03 cm*

Ⓑ *17.03 cm, 17.09 cm, 17.4 cm, 17.31 cm*

Ⓒ *17.4 cm, 17.03 cm, 17.09 cm, 17.31 cm*

Ⓓ *17.03 cm, 17.09 cm, 17.31 cm, 17.4 cm*

39. What is the equivalent decimal number for five hundred twelve thousandths?

Ⓐ 0.512

Ⓑ 0.0512

Ⓒ 5120.

Ⓓ 0.00512

40. Reduce $\frac{14}{98}$ to lowest terms.

Ⓐ $\frac{7}{49}$

Ⓑ $\frac{2}{14}$

Ⓒ $\frac{1}{7}$

Ⓓ $\frac{3}{8}$

Thank You

We at Mometrix would like to extend our heartfelt thanks to you, our friend and patron, for allowing us to play a part in your journey. It is a privilege to serve people from all walks of life who are unified in their commitment to building the best future they can for themselves.

The preparation you devote to these important testing milestones may be the most valuable educational opportunity you have for making a real difference in your life. We encourage you to put your heart into it—that feeling of succeeding, overcoming, and yes, conquering will be well worth the hours you've invested.

We want to hear your story, your struggles and your successes, and if you see any opportunities for us to improve our materials so we can help others even more effectively in the future, please share that with us as well. **The team at Mometrix would be absolutely thrilled to hear from you!** So please, send us an email (support@mometrix.com) and let's stay in touch.

Additional Bonus Material

Due to our efforts to try to keep this book to a manageable length, we've created a link that will give you access to all of your additional bonus material.

Please visit http://www.mometrix.com/bonus948/gmg5math to access the information.